DARE TO FLY

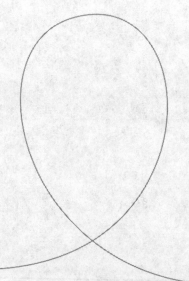

MARTHA McSALLY

wm

WILLIAM MORROW
An Imprint of HarperCollins*Publishers*

DARE TO FLY

Simple Lessons in Never Giving Up

DARE TO FLY. Copyright © 2020 by Martha McSally. Addendum © 2021 by Martha McSally. All rights reserved. Printed in the United States of America. No part of this book may be used or reproduced in any manner whatsoever without written permission except in the case of brief quotations embodied in critical articles and reviews. For information, address HarperCollins Publishers, 195 Broadway, New York, NY 10007.

HarperCollins books may be purchased for educational, business, or sales promotional use. For information, please email the Special Markets Department at SPsales@harpercollins.com.

A hardcover edition of this book was published in 2020 by William Morrow, an imprint of HarperCollins Publishers.

FIRST WILLIAM MORROW PAPERBACK EDITION PUBLISHED 2021.

Library of Congress Cataloging-in-Publication Data has been applied for.

ISBN 978-0-06-299629-9

21 22 23 24 25   LSC   10 9 8 7 6 5 4 3 2 1

To all those who choose to live "in the arena." To the pioneers before us, who dared greatly, and those with the courage and strength to follow. Above all, to all the men and women in uniform who gave their lives so that we may live in freedom.

66It is not the critic who counts; not the man who points out how the strong man stumbles, or where the doer of deeds could have done them better. The credit belongs to the man who is actually in the arena, whose face is marred by dust and sweat and blood; who strives valiantly; who errs, who comes short again and again . . . who knows great enthusiasms, the great devotions; who spends himself in a worthy cause; who at the best knows in the end the triumph of high achievement, and who at the worst, if he fails, at least fails while daring greatly, so that his place shall never be with those cold and timid souls who neither know victory nor defeat.99

—THEODORE ROOSEVELT, 1910

(I found this quote in a book while I was a cadet at the Air Force Academy and have carried my copy with me ever since.)

Contents

ONE

Cleared
to Fly

*"Stop waiting for the perfect
moment, the perfect set of
conditions, and the perfect answer."*

I WAS STRAPPED INSIDE THE cockpit of an A-10 attack plane, affectionately dubbed "the Warthog" by its pilots, with my feet clamped on the brakes. The only thing racing faster than the engines was my heart. I was an experienced Air Force aviator, but I had never flown *this* airplane. My first time airborne in a Warthog would be when I lifted it— solo—off the ground.

The last of the A-10 Warthogs rolled off the assembly line in 1984, the year I graduated high school. It was built to be an attack plane, flying low to the ground. I didn't have a clue what it felt like to take off in one because we had no two-seat training planes and no simulators. Instead, we used what was called a "cockpit familiarization trainer." It consisted of a regular office chair surrounded by a mock cockpit, outfitted with the panels and switches found inside the airplane—except none of the switches did anything and the gauges didn't work. Listening to the engines roar and watching the southern Arizona sun glint off the A-10's metal skin, I did not feel like I was sitting in an office chair.

In minutes, the tower would clear me for takeoff. This is absolutely crazy, I thought.

My instructor pilot was waiting in an adjacent airplane. His job was to "chase" me by flying close and instructing me over the radio. But only I could fly my plane. I radioed the tower, gave my call sign, and said, "Ready for takeoff runway 30." Tower replied, Winds are 310 at 8, you are cleared for takeoff. Obviously, no one was going to come to their senses. The runway was all mine. I taxied out.

With the engines fully engaged and my muscles straining, I ran the final instrument and system checks.

There were no more preparations. The next motion would be to go. I said a short prayer, very popular with pilots throughout more than one hundred years of human flight, which can be paraphrased as "God, please don't let me mess up!" I took my feet off the brakes and started barreling down the runway. At 115 miles per hour, all looked good. At about 166 mph, the aircraft lifted off the ground. Within seconds, I was flying at 230 miles per hour. In my tanks, I had enough fuel to last about two hours. There was, however, one small nagging concern: just as I had never taken off in a Warthog, I had also never landed one. Instructor pilots are fond of joking with their trainees: "Don't worry too much. You've got the rest of your life to figure out how to get this plane back on the ground." That day, the joke was on me.

I SUFFERED FROM MOTION SICKNESS as a little girl, so I would have laughed at anyone who predicted I would grow up to be the first U.S. woman to fly a fighter jet in combat. I was a quiet, tomboyish kid, hardly the type of person who would spend eight years fighting for the rights of women in uniform, ultimately suing the Pentagon—and winning. I was a pudgy, shy adolescent, and my siblings would have bet with certainty that I would never become an accomplished athlete, or win triathlons, or climb the highest mountains in Africa and western Europe. Or that when my right hand was broken at the Air Force Academy, I would spend months relearning not only how to write but also how to throw a javelin with my left. I hung up my pilot wings and left the military in part because it was too political, yet I served in the U.S. Senate.

The one thing that has made my life turn out differently from what I expected is that I stopped waiting for the perfect moment, the perfect set of conditions, and the perfect answer.

I could fill an entire page with buzzwords and stock phrases about how I should have matched my dreams with reality, managed my expectations, or not bitten off more than I could chew. After all, if I was afraid of heights, I would not have been a great candidate to become a fighter pilot, no matter how much I wanted to fly. But the real truth is: everyone has dreams. So, we should dream big ones. As the Air Force motto says, Aim High. We only get one shot at this life.

However, it doesn't stop with the dream. In fact, the dream is only the start. We need to be prepared to fight for our dreams, to refuse to give up. Most things worth doing are not achieved without a struggle or without periods of intense uncertainty, frustration, fatigue, fear, and even fierce opposition. But so often that makes their accomplishment more rewarding, not less. When faced with a roadblock, get creative. If my life is emblematic of anything, it is the determination to seek a new route, an unconventional option, a fresh way forward.

I HAD ZERO DESIRE TO fly when I applied to the Air Force Academy for college. I knew very little about the military. Even though my late father had served in the Navy, I didn't grow up listening to his Navy stories, we didn't live near a military base, and I don't recall meeting anyone in uniform before I applied to the academy. My plan was to become a doctor so I could save other children's fathers. Going to a service academy meant that my widowed mother wouldn't have to try to pay for college and medical school.

Once I got to the academy, my thinking began to change. From the start, women and men completed the same instruction and drills. But even when the women performed better than their male classmates, they were denied fighter and bomber pilot assignments, solely because they were female. It was the law! I was blessed to have grown up in a home where I was told I could be anything I wanted, with no limitations because I was a girl. My parents encouraged all five McSally kids to work hard and achieve our potential. Only *after* I joined the military was I exposed to biases toward women and learned about sexism and gender discrimination. Discovering that I couldn't become a fighter pilot just because I was female really ticked me off. But I channeled my feisty, rebellious spirit in a positive way; I began to dream about becoming a fighter pilot to prove "them" wrong.

The summer between sophomore and junior year at the academy, every cadet spends three weeks at a base to see "the real Air Force." It could be a missile base in Wyoming or a "forward" base halfway around the world. I was fortunate to draw Torrejón Air Base, outside Madrid, Spain. I spent time with the F-16 squadron and rode in the back seat for a few training flights, never getting motion sickness and loving every minute in the air. I also observed the military doctors at the base hospital. Any remaining questions I had about my future were answered during that trip. Although I am thankful for the amazing medical professionals who serve in uniform, it was increasingly clear to me that I "belonged" as a pilot. I decided to apply for flight school, with medical school as my fallback.

At the academy, I was chosen to be the first female cadet in charge of the Assault Course, where cadets learn the basics of hand-to-hand combat. The course is physically and mentally exhausting, and I found it the most challenging part of basic training. The course culminates in a pugil stick fight, which is basically like trying to beat up your opponent using a broomstick wrapped in heavy pads. (For civilians, there are backyard versions called "inflatable joust games," and you can buy them online.)

While I was working, Lieutenant General Charles Hamm, the superintendent of the Air Force Academy, and his wife, Jane, visited. I looked up to the general and his wife. During a break, she asked my plans after graduation. I told her I was premed, but felt a strong urge to become a pilot, with the dream of becoming a fighter pilot. She told me to trust my gut.

That was the last nudge I needed. I withdrew from the medical school application process and told my commanding officer I was going all-in on pilot training. There was only one "small" problem: I was slightly too short to qualify for pilot training for any plane, let alone fighters.

MANY PEOPLE ASPIRE TO BECOME pilots, only to have their dreams dashed because they lack 20/20 vision or have a heart murmur that is discovered during the flight physical. Following my initial medical screening in school for the academy, I was told that I was not "pilot-qualified" due to my height, but I didn't care because I wasn't planning on flying.

Now I did. I underwent another physical and passed in every area, except for my total height. My sitting height was acceptable, but the minimum total height to fly was five feet four inches, and I was about five feet three and a half on a good day. At first, I was determined to get to five foot four. After discovering that the spine compresses during the day,

I bought a pair of gravity boots and hung upside down from a pull-up bar in my dorm's stairwell. I even half seriously asked a buddy to hit me on the head, explaining that a well-placed bump would get me over the top. My gravity-defying efforts gained me a quarter inch, not enough.

Height standards are important. If a pilot isn't tall enough to clearly see over the instrument panel during a rough landing or can't easily look back behind the jet to see an enemy plane or missile, that pilot has a problem. For leg length, the issue is whether the pilot can slam on the pedals hard enough to break a spin, make an emergency landing, or abort a take-off after a blown tire or brake failure. There are also upper limits on pilot height. If the pilot's sitting height is too tall, the aircraft canopy cannot close properly. If a pilot's legs are too long, they can be severed during an ejection. Combat airplanes are built for male bodies in the middle of the bell curve. Lots of women (and some men) are disqualified from flying because they aren't the right size.

I was, however, told that medical waivers were granted if you were within one inch of the height cutoff, short or tall, as long as you could pass a cockpit fitting and were recommended by both a flight surgeon and an instructor pilot (the flight surgeon even noted on my form that I had "overpowered" both him and the instructor pilot on the rudder pedals). I had passed the cockpit fittings in two aircraft; I had all my recommendations. I thought I was an excellent waiver candidate.

Months later, my package came back stamped DENIED, with no explanation.

I WASN'T ALONE IN MY quest; the academy's clinic commander, Colonel Christopher Bell, was firmly in my corner. After the first denial, he sent my package back, requesting reconsideration. The bureaucracy answered again: DENIED. When Colonel Bell asked for a reason, he was told that several pilots, after receiving waivers for being too short, had skidded off the runway during aborted takeoffs, damaging their planes. The investigators blamed the accidents on pilot height. Now, 100 percent of the waiver requests from "short pilot" candidates were being denied—although they still had all of us "shorties" complete cockpit fittings, getting our hopes up. That's when I first learned how callous and irrational bureaucracies can be.

Even more galling was how arbitrary this process was. I watched a talented football player fail the cockpit test because he was too tall to safely close the plane's canopy. The flight surgeon and instructor pilots all recommended "denial of flight clearance," but instead the same bureaucracy approved his waiver and sent him to pilot training.

I was incensed. I vented to Colonel Bell, "So let me get this straight: I was cleared to fly medically. I passed the cockpit fittings and got my approvals. Yet some bureaucrat is overriding all that and killing my dream? That is ridiculous. Where are these people? Let's go talk to them!" I am not sure whether Colonel Bell wanted me to go away or was annoyed that his recommendations were being discounted, or a combination. But he embarked on a creative solution.

Since I was a varsity swimmer and had started to compete in triathlons and marathons, he proposed we make a case that my leg strength was above average, and that would more than compensate. He devised a study to compare my leg strength to a group of pilot-qualified cadets, male and female. My leg strength tested above average for male athletes and well above average overall. Again, Colonel Bell argued for my waiver. We felt confident. We sent the revised package off and waited.

The fall of my senior year, I was summoned to see Colonel Bell. He told me it was over, my package had been denied for a third time. I was initially stunned and transitioned quickly into being angry. Really angry. Faceless bureaucrats were taking the path of least resistance, rather than looking at individual circumstances and applying judgment. They had not seen a leg-strength argument before, so they played it safe and rejected it. Colonel Bell said he was sorry, but it was time for me to consider other career paths. *My dream was officially dead.*

I left his office in disbelief. The walk to my dorm was one of the heaviest walks of my life. I wanted to scream, cry, and throw things. By the time I reached my room, I simply felt crushed. After nearly three and a half years of working to excel at the academy, I would never be a pilot because my legs were half an inch too short.

A couple of minutes after I walked out, General Hamm walked into the clinic. He stuck his head in Colonel Bell's office to say hello. The colonel was still smarting from our conversation. General Hamm asked what was wrong, and the colonel explained that for many months, he had been fighting to get a waiver for one cadet, and he finally had to tell the cadet it was over, she would never fly. General Hamm asked who it was. When he learned the cadet was me, he offered to take my package to the head of Air Training Command. He told Colonel Bell, "If we can't get her a waiver, I will ask him for an exception to policy. McSally is going to fly."

I was moping in my room when someone knocked on the door and said I had a phone call. Colonel Bell sounded jubilant and explained what had happened. That night, I thanked God for hearing my prayers and for creating a world where even generals need Band-Aids and checkups.

General Hamm succeeded.

The waiver letter from then-Lieutenant General John Shaud stated, "The successful cockpit evaluations together with her academic and athletic accomplishments certainly outweigh the minor height defect. Therefore, I will make an exception in her case. Please advise Captain McSally . . . and extend my best wishes for her success as a pilot in our United States Air Force."

You would think that would be the happy ending. But there was another twist in the road.

IN PILOT TRAINING, THERE IS a saying that if you want to stay out of trouble in the air, "don't do anything dumb, dangerous, or different." I hadn't made it into the air yet, but I managed to do something different, dangerous, and dumb on the ground.

Pranks before football games were fairly common among the service academies. During my junior year, Annapolis midshipmen changed the huge letters on our football stadium that spelled AIR FORCE to read NAVY. It took a lot of scrambling to return it to AIR FORCE before kickoff. My senior year, we were slated to play West Point at home. I decided to do something different: I led my freshmen cadets on a nighttime campout by the stadium in case the Army cadets got any similar ideas. My commander made it clear if there was any trouble, we were to call security, and he would hold me accountable for any altercations. No West Pointers appeared, but there were several campers parked nearby—before 9/11, anyone could drive onto the academy grounds. One guy in a camper, who was clearly inebriated or on drugs, became belligerent and was harassing my freshmen.

Knowing my butt was on the line, instead of calling campus security, I tried to de-escalate the situation myself—dangerous. The guy was irrationally shouting about being the world champion finger wrestler, and it was clear to me that he wouldn't budge until we "finger wrestled." I agreed on the condition that he would get back in his RV. I held up my right hand—dumb. He grabbed it and twisted both our hands, hard. I felt a bit of pain, but I pulled my hand away and told him we were done.

My hand hurt, but it didn't feel like anything was broken. It was a cold night in November, which helped minimize swelling. Morning came, and I left Colorado to lead a cadet team to Washington, D.C., to run the Marine Corps marathon. During the flight, I realized he had done real damage to the middle finger on my right hand. I went to the emergency room, where the doctor confirmed my finger was broken in a few places. He immobilized my hand in a bulky brace up to my elbow and put my entire arm in a sling.

The next morning, I started the marathon with my fellow cadets but had no intention of completing the race. I had been up nearly all night, two nights in a row, and was wearing a sling. It was my first time in D.C., and I was awestruck by the monuments and sights along the route. As my feet kept moving, I gazed, wide-eyed, at the Capitol, the White House, the Lincoln Memorial, and all the other amazing monuments. I forgot about my injury and my lack of sleep. The next thing I knew, I was running up the hill to the Marine Corps Memorial. Having completed more than twenty miles, I decided to finish the race. I'm pretty sure my final time was the fastest I have ever posted in more than a dozen marathons.

At the academy, I saw an orthopedist for a follow-up. He

confirmed my finger was broken but removed the immobilizer and said it just needed to be "buddy taped" to the next finger to heal. Weeks later, on a visit home to Rhode Island, I showed my hand with its now very crooked finger to our neighbor, an orthopedist, who for years had put the McSally kids back together. He took X-rays and told me I needed surgery.

Sure enough, another Air Force physician agreed. I had three surgeries in the next two years. Finally, a fourth surgery, which removed the damaged tendon in my middle finger and replaced it with the extra tendon from my index finger, succeeded. My finger still looked funny and I couldn't straighten it all the way, but on the tests, my right hand functioned as well as my left.

I scheduled my flight physical. It was my last chance. If I wasn't cleared to fly, the Air Force would automatically send me on another career track. Functionally, I had no limitations. The flight doctor completed his evaluation and agreed, but he added that my finger wasn't perfect. And I needed to be perfect to receive my initial flying clearance.

To me, this rationale made no sense. Once you become a pilot, you can have all sorts of medical problems, go nearly blind (as long as it is correctable to 20/20), be on certain medicines for chronic conditions, and that is okay. But to become a pilot, you have to be perfect. He picked up his pen and was about to write on my medical clearance form. Again, I felt my dreams dying, based on the whims of one officer. I couldn't let it happen. I had come too far to give up now.

Impulsively, I decided to demonstrate to this flight doctor just how well my finger could function. I reached over with my right hand and pinched him as hard as I could on the fleshy part of his side with my bad middle finger and my thumb. He nearly jumped out of his chair. I finally let go and held my hand close to his face. "What do you need me to do with this finger, Doc, to prove that I am capable of being a pilot?" I asked, raising my voice. "What else do you want me to do? I have been through four brutal years at the Air Force Academy, had four surgeries on my hand because of the incompetent military doc who let my finger heal crooked, spent two years in and out of casts and physical therapy. I have done everything I can to make sure I am qualified to fly, and all the test results you have in front of you prove that I can. And you are going to take this dream away from me with the stroke of your pen just because you say it isn't perfect? What do you want me to do with this finger to show you that I can fly?"

I will never forget the look on his face—shocked, amused, and maybe even impressed at the strength of my finger. He picked up his pen, stared at my form, and hesitated for what seemed like an eternity. Finally, he checked the box that said "cleared to fly" and signed his name.

I WAS SLATED TO BEGIN pilot training in August 1990. Less than six months later, the U.S. was officially at war.

On August 2, Iraq invaded Kuwait, took control of the

country, and declared it to be the nineteenth Iraqi province. By mid-January, the United States and a coalition of allied nations were fighting to expel Iraq's troops.

The U.S. military deployed more than thirty-seven thousand women to the Middle East for Operations Desert Shield and Desert Storm. Although women served only in "combat support" roles, fifteen servicewomen were killed and two became prisoners of war. This prompted a fresh debate about women in combat, and ultimately Congress voted to repeal the law that prohibited women from becoming combat pilots. I was ranked fifth in my pilot-training class, placing me on track to become a combat pilot—when I graduated, General Hamm gave me *his* pilot wings to wear, which I treasure to this day.

But although Congress had repealed the law, it did not require any of the military services to change their policies, and they didn't.

All the services were being downsized following the collapse of the Soviet Union. The Air Force disbanded entire flying squadrons and could not absorb the new pilots graduating from training. To solve this problem, the Air Force initiated what it called the "banked pilot" program. It put pilots in "the bank" and placed them in desk jobs for a few years, with a plan to "withdraw" them when plane assignments became available. Fifty-five percent of my pilot-training class did not receive flying assignments upon graduation. Instead, they were deposited in "the bank."

I tried to get permission to be put in the bank and wait

for a fighter slot. No surprise, the official response was no, because even though the law said I could be a fighter pilot, current Air Force rules still did not permit women to fly fighter aircraft. My best bet was to become an instructor pilot for the T-38, the supersonic jet used for training. It was considered a top assignment for a woman, and when the Air Force policy changed, I would be ready. When I completed my training, five separate bases were graduating pilots, and there were only two T-38 slots. But I wasn't worried.

At the end of training, pilots selected their assignments much like a sports team draft. We were given a list. Then the five bases got on a conference call and each graduate was asked, based on their class rank, to choose an assignment. The five pilots graduating number one went first, then the twos, and so on, until the assignments were gone and every graduate had made a selection.

On assignment day, my class walked into the wing commander's conference room. All the available aircraft assignments were projected onto a wall screen, plus all the "banked" pilot slots. We sat in chairs along the wall, in order by class rank. Those chairs formed a classic bell curve of stress; graduates at the top of the class knew they could select what they wanted, while those at the bottom knew they could not. For the middle, the choices could go either way.

All the bases had performed a dry run of selections so the graduates would be prepared. No one in front of me at any base had chosen a T-38 assignment. Knowing that, I didn't even look at the rest of the list before I walked into the official selection meeting. As someone who normally plans and even overplans for contingencies, this was a big mistake on my part.

The process was the same for each pilot: you wrote your choice on an index card, walked up, saluted the wing commander, and handed him your card. He then announced the pick on the conference call. An aide would cross out that assignment, and the next candidate would rise.

After two rounds, the selections had gone as planned. Then the pilot graduating third in our group stood. Seconds before handing over his index card, he took it back, crossed off his choice and wrote something else. The wing commander announced: "T-38 to Reese." What? He had chosen one of the two T-38 slots—the slot I had planned to pick.

He sat down and my buddy, who was number four, asked him, "What happened? Why did you change your mind?" He answered, "I have wanted to be a fighter pilot since I was a little boy. I stood there ready to hand over the card requesting a cargo plane and realized that I was ending my chances to become a fighter pilot."

Now it was pilot number four's turn. He walked to the commander and hesitated. Then he crossed out his choice and wrote something new. The wing commander announced: "T-38 to Vance." Everyone in the class looked at me. He had just chosen the last T-38 slot.

I was in shock. I hadn't considered any other assignments since no one had been planning to pick them, and T-38s were never chosen that high in a class unless it was a woman doing the selecting. He sat down and said something like, "Sorry, Martha, I need to keep my options open, too!" He had every right to pick that plane, but now all eyes were on me.

I could still keep my dream alive by choosing to become a T-37 instructor pilot. The T-37 was a very old, noisy, two-seat plane used for the first six months of pilot training. It was nowhere near as capable as the T-38. T-37 instructors had to do the heavy lifting of turning "pedestrians into pilots," including weeding out potential flyers who suffer from airsickness or lack of judgment in dangerous situations. It was a tough job. I could also pick a transport or tanker aircraft; there were several still available in locations around the world. I could choose a great place with a good quality of life.

I read through the listings glowing on the overhead projector as I approached the wing commander. Out of frustration, I wrote down a C-130 to Ramstein, Germany. It's over, I thought, just go fly a cool cargo plane in Germany. Then a graduate at another base selected the C-130 to Ramstein. It was gone.

I had no idea what to do as my commander, classmates, and four other bases waited for me to decide. I wrote a few choices, then pulled the card back, sensing I was making a bad decision. Finally, I took a deep breath and resigned myself to the fact that my best option was the dreaded T-37. Now I needed to pick a base: Columbus, Mississippi; Enid, Oklahoma; or Laughlin, in Del Rio, Texas. I had lived in

Arizona for a year, and after growing up in New England, I wanted to be in a warm climate. I remembered hearing that Del Rio had a nice lake. I handed over my card. "T-37 to Laughlin." You could hear a gasp in the room and on the conference call. Who in their right mind graduating fifth in the class would pick a T-37 to Laughlin Air Force Base?

I sat down and tried to process what had happened. I had made a monumental choice about the direction in my life with almost no forethought and under extraordinary stress. I remember thinking, I busted my butt and pulled all-nighters for four years at the academy to become a Distinguished Graduate, followed by two challenging years at Harvard graduate school getting a master's degree, and a year of hard work at pilot training, only to end up flying a plane I don't want to fly in a place I don't want to live. What a failure. Doubts whirled through my mind: I should have tried harder. I shouldn't have mouthed off to the flight commander, whose rating had lowered my final class rank. I should have chosen another cargo plane.

After assignment day, the wing commander summoned me to his office to discuss my selection. Before I could speak, he said I had made the absolute best decision possible. He said that as he watched me agonize, he wanted so badly to advise me to pick a T-37. He believed the restriction on women fighter pilots would be lifted in the next few years, and the T-37 would allow me to build my experience and overall airmanship while I waited for a fighter assignment. Had I chosen a cargo or air-refueling plane, there would be no way to cross over. He was so proud that I had the foresight and determination to keep going. Well, at least I had determination!

The pep talk encouraged me, but it wasn't easy. I remember driving from Phoenix to Del Rio, stopping my car in the pouring rain, pulling out my briefcase, and looking at all the other assignments, the ones I had rejected. I was filled with regret.

I second-guessed myself for a while. But I discovered that I loved teaching, and I grew to love Del Rio, Texas, where the community was devoted to its base and to pilot training. And Lake Amistad is a beautiful lake. Many days, I would walk out the door of my townhouse and dive in to swim. Then, in April 1993, I received a phone call from a general at the Pentagon. He said he was aware that I had tried to pick a banked fighter assignment at the end of my pilot training and was wondering, "Are you still interested in being a fighter pilot?"

My response was, "Yes! I chose to fly T-37s. What do you think?" He explained that the Pentagon was preparing to lift the ban, and the Air Force had identified seven women, who based on their training, class rank, and current assignments, were eligible to become the service's first fighter pilots. They had vetted us to see if we could withstand the scrutiny of being pioneers. The last step was to ask if we still wanted the opportunity. I would have to fly to Washington the next day to prepare for press conferences and interviews, and I couldn't tell anyone except my commander.

My fellow pilots had overheard my end of the conversation and looked at me as I put down the phone. But the general had said I couldn't talk. With a grin on my face, I said, "Wrong number." I fooled exactly no one. My dream was alive!

Looking back, if I hadn't taken that T-37 to Del Rio, if I hadn't given my all to a noisy, hot plane and to my students, some of whom puked all over me and the cockpit (stories for another time!), I never would have gotten the phone call and the opportunity that truly changed my life. Even if things seemed unfair, I resisted the temptation to carry a chip on my shoulder. Instead, I resolved to put my head down and give 110 percent. I didn't know what I was going to do next or where this would lead, but I knew at the very least I'd be ready.

We can all find our own "T-37 to Del Rio" and excel on the pathway toward our dreams.

TWO

Make Someone Proud

"Treat every day as a gift."

ONE OF MY FONDEST MEMORIES is of digging for clams with my father in the shallow inlets dotting the coast around Matunuck, Rhode Island. We would ride to the clamming area in our little dinghy, anchor the boat, and use our feet and rakes to find the quahogs, usually just below the surface of the sand. My dad worked long hours, chaired the local school committee, and had five kids, so there were few times for us to simply "be."

The grandson of Irish immigrants, Bernard F. McSally was born into challenging circumstances in upstate New York. His father died before he was born; his mother passed away when he was a teenager. Of his six siblings, three died young from the various illnesses and diseases that plagued families in the 1920s and '30s—two had passed away before he was born. None of his three remaining siblings went to college, but they all worked hard to provide for their families. My dad started working at age eight and never stopped.

After high school, he joined the Naval Reserve and worked multiple jobs, including as a comanager at a gas station. His boss was a Notre Dame graduate and pushed my dad to apply. He finally did and was accepted. The workers at other service stations took up a collection and raised $73.50 to help send him on his way. Dad broke down and cried when they presented him with the money. His sisters also pooled what little they had, and Dad worked during school and every summer. A job at the student hangout, "The Huddle," was how he met Regis Philbin, later a famous entertainer and talk show host. After my dad's death, Regis wrote that Bernard McSally "was one of those unforgettable guys who made a terrific impact on me as a young man."

My father graduated from Notre Dame in 1952 and stayed to earn a master's degree in corrections administration in 1953.

Upon graduation, Dad was commissioned as an officer in the United States Navy. I still have an old, yellowed newspaper clipping of him being named an "honor recruit" in 1953. A year later, Dad met and fell in love with Eleanor Taft, while he attended training and she was in college in Newport, Rhode Island. He was sent to sea as part of a crew assigned to map key ocean areas during the Cold War. Eleanor waited for him, and they wed in 1957. After four years of active duty in the Navy, Dad worked for the prison system in New York, then Massachusetts, and used the GI Bill to attend Boston College Law School at night. When he graduated in 1962, he was already a father of three. My oldest brother, Mark, was born in 1958, followed by Michael in 1959, Martin in 1962, and Mary Kaitlin in 1964. I was the baby, born in 1966. By then, our family had moved to Rhode Island, and my father practiced law with my mom's brother, Jim.

Even as a successful lawyer, Dad was humble, modest,

and frugal. My brother Michael remembers that he used to cut his old suit trousers into shorts and wear them with his old wingtip shoes and a white T-shirt to mow the lawn on the weekends. He always drove crappy cars. His clients gave him a hard time, saying he made them look bad by driving those old beaters around. He was generous and compassionate. Once, after minor surgery at our local hospital, he was placed in a room with a man whose family was clearly struggling. Dad sent a handwritten note and an envelope of cash to the hospital's president, asking him to share the money anonymously to ensure his former roommate and his family had a full Christmas. Dad didn't want anyone to know who had given the gift. He just wanted that man's family to be blessed.

Like many in their generation, my father worked long hours and my mom stayed home to be the CEO of our house and the kids. We lived in a nice neighborhood in Warwick, Rhode Island, and in 1968, my parents bought a beach house forty-five minutes away. From the time I could walk and talk, I spent every summer in Matunuck. A little village, Matunuck had a small oceanfront divided into public and private beach areas, clubs, private dwellings, and a trailer park. Our wonderful house had stone pillars and a big backyard, and was located about two hundred yards from the beach. It sat on the end of Potter Pond. If you traveled far enough through the water, you could be carried all the way to the Atlantic.

Many days, I grabbed a net and caught blue crabs for

lunch. We dug our own clams from the nearby sand flats or caught minnows off our dock and sold them as bait fish for candy money. My brothers fished for bluefish and flounder and set lobster traps out in the breakwater; later, they worked on commercial fishing boats. My dad did some fishing, but he preferred digging for clams. He was the one who sent us to collect mussels, easy to pick from the reef at low tide. Mussels were not popular at the time, but Dad would skillfully prepare a batch of mussels marinara for his hungry brood. We had many perfect summer weekends at the beach, swimming and playing in the water, building sandcastles, and relaxing in the sun.

On Sunday, August 6, 1978, my older brothers, Mark and Michael, were home from college, and we spent the day at the beach. Afterward, I remember my father went upstairs to lie down, saying he wasn't feeling well, which was unusual. I went outside to play and when I came in, I was told that Mark had driven Dad to the hospital with my mom.

When I heard my dad was at the hospital, I don't remember being afraid or even particularly concerned. I didn't know anyone who had died. I assumed the doctors would make him better and everything would be fine.

My mom came home that night and sat us down, explaining that my father had suffered a heart attack. She said that he was recovering and was in stable condition. We would all need to help care for him once he was released from the hospital. I listened to Mom, but I didn't even know what a heart attack was. I was just focused on having my dad be around more and being able to help him.

I went to bed, and sometime in the middle of the night, I was startled awake by one of my brothers, barking at me to "get up right now and go to the car." I was confused, but I got dressed and headed downstairs. In the car, I asked what was going on. They told me we were going to see Dad. I didn't understand why we couldn't wait until morning, but no one said anything more. So, as the youngest of the five, I kept my questions to myself and my mouth shut. (It was probably one of the few times in my life that I did.)

My brother Mark drove the seven or eight miles to South County Hospital in a blinding rainstorm. Water flooded the roads, whipped by strong winds. After we finally reached the hospital, we spent time with my dad as a family and individually.

As a twelve-year-old, those hours were very surreal to me. My brother Michael recalls Dad confidently telling everyone that he was leaving us and that he was at peace. Dad was very specific and steadfast with his message: I am going to die. God is real, and I can sense Him. And there is a life after death, I can feel it.

In my time alone with my dad, I could not believe that this might be the last time I would talk to him, so I didn't feel the need to say everything I would have wanted to say. Instead, we spoke about school, about the stray beagle named Hobo we had taken in and loved for years as our family dog until he disappeared a few months earlier. We talked about swimming. (I had taken up competitive swimming in elementary school, partly because my brothers told me I was chubby and needed to lose weight.) Then my dad told me that I had a bright future. He added, "I want you to make me proud." Of course, Daddy, I promised. I said goodbye, kissed him, and left him to get some rest.

The sun came up, and the doctors assured us my dad was stable, so we headed home to rest. I don't remember how many hours passed before the phone rang, and we were told to return to the hospital. When we arrived, we were told that Dad had suffered a second heart attack and had died. I initially refused to believe it. I had just been talking to him, and he was fine. If I could see him again, I was sure I could prove them wrong.

My dad was only forty-nine years old. At the time, I thought that was pretty old, but now that I have passed forty-nine, I am aware of how early it is to be snatched from this earth. We trooped in to say a final goodbye to his body, already stiff and cold. His spirit was long gone. Then we left the hospital, and my life has never been the same.

I learned much later that the reason we rushed to the hospital in the middle of the night was that my father had insisted to the medical staff that we be summoned because he knew in his spirit he was going to die, and he was adamant that he needed to see his family one last time. The doctor had tried to reassure us, saying Dad would be fine, that it was normal for people to react this way after a major health scare. My dad was a man of faith, and I am grateful he followed God's prompting, which gave us a chance to spend that final bit of time with him. I also do believe that when he said he was "at peace," those were not mere words. My dad was remarkably peaceful in the middle of that night, and I believe his deep faith and a sense of being surrounded by God's spirit gave him the comfort to know that he was leaving us to be with the Lord.

I don't remember much about the next few days, except lots of people coming in and out of our home and how nothing could stop the screaming in my soul. I had moments when I "forgot" that my dad was gone. I would look down the driveway, expecting him to pull in, home for dinner. Then I would remember that he was dead.

I had spent a week in July at sleepaway camp. In previous years when I came home, I would kiss my mom and dad an extra good night for all the nights I had missed while at camp. But this year, I had yet to make up all the kisses. I became obsessed with giving Dad his remaining kisses before he was buried. Each night, I kissed the air, trying to reach his spirit, but I worried he would not receive the kisses if I didn't give them to his body. At his wake, I told a relative that I needed to give my father his missing kisses. After the guests departed, I kissed the earthly, cold shell of my father seven final times.

The wake lasted for hours. The line for visitors stretched out the door and for several blocks. His funeral was the same, standing room only, the crowd spilling out of the church doors. The city lowered its flags to half-staff in his honor, and police officers from three different communities escorted his casket to convey thanks and recognition for Dad's selfless service. Dozens of strangers waited in the receiving lines to talk to us and share their stories of how Dad had helped them in ways small and large.

I hated the wake and the funeral. I hated standing in the receiving line watching total strangers cry and carry on. I did not want them to hug me. They might miss him, but they would move on with their lives. I had lost my father forever.

School started a few weeks later. It was my first year at Aldrich Junior High School. I remember looking around the bus and thinking, "He has a father, she has a father, he has a father . . . Why am I the only one that doesn't have a father? Why? Why?"

My two oldest brothers returned to college, my third brother and my sister were in high school, and my mom decided to channel her grief into action. She immediately enrolled in school to get her master's degree so she could lead our family and pursue a career in education. Mom was forty-four, a widow, and a single parent with five kids. Today, I can't even imagine how alone and abandoned she must have felt. I am grateful she found a way to put one foot in front of the other and put her needs aside. For years, I gave her cards at Mother's Day and Father's Day, because I knew she was playing both roles. When I graduated high school, I presented her with an engraved trophy, my thank-you to her for seeing me through and putting up with me. But I'm not sure I fully appreciated all that she did or all that she suffered, because I was stuck in my own painful grief. The only words I could hang on to were my father's last ones: "make me proud."

In the darkest and most difficult times of my life, I often found my last ounce of strength to persevere while thinking about my dad and his request. During pilot training, when I was strapped into a parachute harness and dragged across open water by a boat on my stomach and my back to learn how to survive after ejecting, I would think of my dad and how he taught me to be safe in the water. When vile words were said to my face simply because I was a female pilot, I would think of my dad and what kind of officer I know he was. When I see a person or a dog in need, I think of how my dad would have helped them and choose to lend a hand. When I have faced tragic, senseless death and despair, I have reached back to my dad and his words. They were powerful, as was my mom's wordless example of putting her own grief and needs aside to provide for our family.

By the time I reached the Air Force Academy, I recognized another truth from the loss of my dad: treat every day as a gift. Losing my dad at such a young age propelled me to make decisions, particularly big ones, in the context of the fragility of life. Time and again, I have asked myself, "If this were the last day, week, or year of my life, is this the best way for me to spend it?" In my first general election, running for Congress in Arizona, I finished election night thirteen hundred votes ahead. But thousands of ballots remained to be counted. The final count took another fourteen days.

As the presumed winner, I flew to Washington, D.C., for freshman orientation. I was in the freshman photo, voted for the GOP leadership, and attended all the briefings and events. But each day, the ballot count brought more bad news. When the count finished, I had lost by 2,454 votes out of almost 300,000 cast, or .84 percent. If I had convinced 1,228 more people to vote for me instead of my opponent, I would have become Representative McSally. Almost as soon as that 2012 race was over, people encouraged me to run again for 2014. At first, I rebuffed them. I had to think not only whether working long hours nearly every day, putting my personal life on hold, spending down my savings, and getting lied about and denigrated was truly the best way for me to serve. But I also had to think, if these are the last two years of my life, it this the best way for me to spend them to make a difference? (I ended up deciding yes.)

MORE THAN FORTY YEARS AFTER his death, Mom shared a letter that my dad wrote to her before they were married. It was filled with his family and personal history and his desires and thoughts. In the letter, my dad talked about what he wanted in life. "I don't want to get rich; I don't even want to work hard at <u>trying</u> to get rich. Work hard, I will, but not at that goal! I don't want success in the way the word is usually used . . . I don't want my kids working afternoons and evenings in high school. Ellie, I want to make a mark—I want to do something—I want to give something—not that I have very much to give, that's not important. I don't want to do something big that they put you down in history for. I'm not that much of a dreamer; and I'm not that big of a man. I'm one of the little people, one of the vast mob of mediocrity, but I want to do some little thing big. After I've gone to my 'reward,' I want just one bystander to say: 'He was here.' I think I want to help people in some little way . . ."

My eyes are filled with tears as I type this. My dad succeeded in his mission. People from all walks of life said, "He was here." He helped so many others. And he worked himself literally to death to provide a better life and opportunity for my siblings and me. For all of that, I am eternally grateful, but I miss him dearly every day.

THREE

Fight's On!

"Real courage is shown when a
bystander decides to step up and
refuses to tolerate behavior that he or
she knows is wrong."

I KNEW BEFORE I TRANSITIONED to fighter planes in 1994 that I probably wasn't going to be welcomed with open arms. My graduating class at the Air Force Academy was only the ninth to have female cadets; there was only one other woman in my pilot-training class; and during the two and a half years I spent as an instructor pilot, I was the only woman in my group—and my primary job was to teach men how to fly. So I was already familiar with the challenges of being a woman in a very male-dominated institution. Sadly, much of the ambivalence, or downright hostility, surrounding female combat pilots started at the top. The Air Force chief of staff, four-star general Merrill McPeak, was well known for his very public stance against women fighter pilots. During testimony before the U.S. Senate Armed Services Committee, he conveyed that he preferred a less qualified male fighter pilot to a more qualified female, adding, "I have a very traditional attitude about wives and mothers and daughters being ordered to kill people."

My first A-10 operational squadron commander apparently felt much the same. As the leader, he should have summoned his team to say, "We are welcoming a newly qualified pilot, who went through the same training as us, who will go into combat with us, and who I expect to be received as a full member of our squadron family. And if I hear of any hostility, abuse, or unprofessionalism, I will deal with that behavior swiftly and harshly." Or at least something like that. Instead, my squadron mates later told me that his words to the pilots were essentially, *The worst possible thing is about to happen to our squadron, which has a long history as warriors, brothers, and fighter pilots. We are about to get a woman.* Fortunately, the Air Force sent him to a new assignment before our squadron deployed overseas, and I had fantastic commanders after that. Ironically, during the debate to open fighter planes to women, many fighter pilot men argued that women were too emotional to be fighter pilots. Well, I've never met a more emotional bunch of people than the men who argued against women becoming fighter pilots regardless of their skill and performance!

LIKE MANY YOUNG WOMEN IN male-dominated environments, I learned to succeed by "being one of the guys." From the moment I entered the Air Force Academy, I didn't want to stick out; I wanted to fit in and be part of the team. Harmless pranks were a major part of academy life, a great way to have fun and blow off steam in an otherwise very intense environment, and I became a prankster-in-chief.

My section's commanding officer our freshman year lacked a sense of humor and was a strict disciplinarian. The smallest infraction produced a large response, and one subject that particularly irritated him involved carpeting. Unlike freshmen, sophomores, and juniors, who lived in rooms with bare floors that needed to be buffed and shined, seniors had "carpet privileges." They could install carpet in their rooms, finally trading the buffer for a vacuum cleaner, which made preparing for Saturday morning room inspections much easier. But it was a privilege that could be taken away.

I don't recall what prompted it, but our commander, a major, revoked the carpet privileges for all the seniors in our squadron. They were devastated by what they felt was a disproportionate punishment but followed his order. Just for fun, I convinced my classmates that we should install carpet in the commander's office one night while he was at home. The next morning, he lined all of us up and scolded us as we tried not to smirk. Since I was usually the ringleader, he made me responsible for keeping his new office carpet vacuumed and clean. I followed my orders to the letter, appearing at his office in between classes, before marching to lunch, and before swim practice, ensuring that his carpet was clean and that I was annoying in my dedication to the carpet mission. Eventually, he ordered us to remove the carpet. My next idea was even more inspired: to carpet his parking spot.

When the major arrived the following morning, a bunch of us were watching from an upstairs window and laughing, with tears streaming down our faces. Immediately, I was summoned to the major's office to be yelled at and ordered to keep his parking spot clean and vacuumed. I saluted and reported out. After several days of me asking him to back out his car so I could vacuum his parking space, he gave up and ordered us to remove the carpeting. Shortly thereafter, he restored the seniors' carpet privileges. The seniors were thrilled, and I took away a couple of valuable lessons: First, laughter is a great antidote in stressful, serious situations. Second, fitting in and being one of the guys is a valuable survival and success strategy. So it seemed like a reasonable strategy to apply once again, as I became a fighter pilot.

A huge part of fighter pilot culture is working hard and playing hard, which on its face seems fine, but I soon realized it meant lots of alcohol, profanity, making sexually inappropriate jokes, and singing raunchy bar songs. For decades, this behavior was excused as a way for "jet jockeys" to blow off steam in a high-risk, high-stress profession. Even wonderful family men in their thirties and forties, who loved and honored their wives and daughters, left those values at the door when they entered the fighter pilots' bar—and every fighter squadron I knew had a bar.

In the early 1990s, during the heated debate over female fighter pilots, one of the main dissenting arguments was that our presence would ruin this fighter pilot culture. Opponents argued that the camaraderie and esprit de corps of the male-only environment was crucial to equipping these men to fly into harm's way and face being killed or captured. Women would imperil this environment, and thus place the overall fighter mission at risk.

Among the "crucial aspects of military readiness" that women might disrupt—and these issues were raised with a straight face by the critics of female pilots: Would we make our male colleagues take down the pinup posters behind their desks? Would we stop them from visiting strip clubs when deployed to Las Vegas for a training exercise? Would we ban them from singing songs about rape and lust and big boobs, and making jokes about the carnage of war? Would we file complaints against them for swearing?

When I began fighter training, I decided I would dedicate myself to proving that women could be excellent fighter pilots. I would outstudy, outprepare, and strive to outfly, and outshoot my fellow trainees. I also decided I would go out of my way *not* to change their environment. Instead, I would join them in drinking, swearing, and chewing tobacco. I refused to sing their sexually denigrating songs, but I was quick-witted and had some great, harsh comebacks to put them in their place when needed. As we fighter pilots say at the start of a combat engagement: "Fight's on!"

A key example of my beat-them-at-their-own-game behavior occurred during a competition called "Crud," which is best described as a mix of pool without sticks and tackle football. The game was created by Canadian fighter pilots. Teams run around the table taking shots and "defending" their pool balls, pockets, and table felt. Depending on the rules and the referee, Crud can get pretty physical. I enjoyed playing because I am small and no one expected me to be a threat, but I would lower my center of gravity and lean into the other players. I earned a reputation for being pretty good and aggressive.

My hips, however, paid the price. My hip bones lined up with the height of the pool table, and I developed lots of bruises. During an annual flight physical, the doctor asked me if I was married. When I said no, he followed up with, "Do you have a boyfriend?" I was a little incensed, and I fired back, "Are you hitting on me while I am sitting here naked in a medical gown?" He was taken aback and said, "No, of course not. It is just that you have lots of bruises around your hips. Deep bruises. Old bruises with new bruises on top. So I was wondering if you were in an abusive relationship."

I laughed and said, "Oh, no, those are just from Crud."

"Crud?" he asked.

"Yep." I explained that it was played in the squadron bars or at the officers' club on Friday nights. "Wow," he said. "I need to stop by the club to check it out."

BUT EVEN THOUGH I COULD succeed at Crud, there were definitely times when I felt like a zoo animal. I was the only woman in a flight suit with an A-10 patch on my arm, and that alone was enough to elicit stares and whispers. One night early in my A-10 training, I was at the officers' club with my classmates when an instructor approached us. He was an evaluator pilot, highly experienced, and one of the guys who flew "check rides" to decide whether we measured up. He had been drinking and was talking smack about me and other women being allowed to fly fighters, specifically how he felt that we lacked the competence and skill to make it through. I am confident, Irish, have three older brothers, and after ten years in uniform had experience in dealing with unwelcoming officers, so I was not going to wilt like a flower, but I was also cognizant that this man could flunk me out of training.

Finally, I couldn't continue to listen to his slurs and barbed comments. I asked him exactly what his problem was with me. He started seething that how no matter how badly I performed, he would not be allowed to flunk me because, as he put it, "you don't have balls." He railed about how he would have to lower standards—as if it were a done deal that I would not meet those standards—because of pressure from above.

Now let me say that the military does not have a perfect record of opening new opportunities to women while also ensuring that standards are not lowered to prevent failure. However, these are not simple matters. If a woman comes into a hostile environment and is not given the same opportunities or quality of training and instruction as her male counterparts because of a desire to see her fail, then those in charge need to ensure she isn't being rejected simply to show that women don't belong. This is a huge leadership issue, and leadership has failed on both sides of the pendulum swing—too tough and too easy—in the past. But every situation is unique.

I point-blank asked the instructor whether our commander had actually told him that I could not fail or said that standards had to be lowered if I did. When he began, "No, but . . ." I cut him off and asked whether he had seen any policy guidance that directed him to pass me even if I didn't meet the standards. He said, "No, but . . ." and I cut him off again. Similar to what I had done with that doctor who didn't want to give me my flight clearance, I got in his face and said something to the effect of, Look, flying fighters is serious business. No one—no one—is telling you to lower those standards and risk any of that for me. In fact, if I don't meet the standards, and you don't flunk me, then *you're* the one that doesn't have balls! Don't doom me to failure or success, but instead find the courage to do what you have been entrusted to do and stand by it based on my objective performance. You detest and resent me because of some imaginary pressure you are manufacturing about a hypothetical situation and probably your own insecurities about women joining your boys' club. Get over it and do your [salty pilot phrase] job!

My classmates were mortified. The next week was our first squadron check ride. I am not sure how much the major even remembered of our conversation, but I had a very professional relationship with him during my training. Fortunately for both of us, I did not take either of my check rides with him, but I passed with flying colors.

Some of my choices, however, were a bit more rash. During pilot training, one of my instructor pilots dipped chewing tobacco and talked me into trying it. I had only chewed tobacco once at the Air Force Academy. I pulled many all-nighters to study for tests and exams, invariably after attending a full day of classes, followed by swim or track practice. To make it through, I drank a ridiculous amount of coffee. But one night, I was so sleep-deprived that when a fellow cadet offered me some Copenhagen, saying it would keep me awake, I tried it. It made me dizzy and nauseous, and I spent half the night puking instead of studying.

So, I was a bit leery when my instructor pilot said, "Momma Mac"—that was his nickname for me—"It's about time you and I share a dip together." He gave me some Skoal mint. It didn't make me nauseous, and I felt very awake and alert. I dipped with him from time to time and used it occasionally when I was a T-37 instructor, and later an A-10 pilot, sometimes to wake me up and sometimes just to create cognitive dissonance with the people around me. More than a few men in the officers' club didn't know what to make of a not quite five-foot-four-inch female pilot, aggressively playing Crud with a beer in her hand and a dip in her mouth. For a while I was given the nickname "Little Dipper," a two-fer, referencing my stature and chewing habit.

One night at the officers' club, a new pilot looked at me and said, "Oh, yeah, you are that A-10 chick who dips." Suddenly, I wondered if I dropped dead tomorrow, would the opening line at my memorial service be "Here lies

Martha, the A-10 chick who dipped"? That was not how I wanted to be remembered. I quit that night.

WHEN THE AIR FORCE OPENED up combat jets to women, not all the barriers were about attitudes. One unexpected challenge: How were we going to pee in the plane? This was not an insignificant issue, since my longest combat mission was 9.3 hours and my longest flight over the Atlantic to deploy home was 11.5 hours, plus additional time in the jet on the ground before takeoff and after landing. Pilots also need to drink in the air, because flying dehydrated is dangerous. Male pilots had what were called piddle packs, so I asked what the plan was for a woman, specifically me. My operations officer shrugged his shoulders and said, "Just wear a Depends." I was not going to eject or be shot down, or even climb out the cockpit after a long, successful mission, wearing a diaper! There are methods for women in civilian planes, but military pilot gear is very different. We wear a flight suit, an antigravity suit, a parachute harness, leg straps, a seat belt, and, if we fly across the ocean in cold weather, a rubber suit on top of all of that.

The rigid rubber suits had a heavy, waterproof zipper that ran in a horizontal line just below their belly buttons for the guys to pee. They referred to it as "the jaws of death" because the stiff zipper had to be pried open and if they let go, it would slam shut. But a waist-level horizontal zipper was not an option for a female. I was in my garage looking around for ideas when I had a MacGyver moment. We could turn the inseam stitching on my flight suit into Velcro and then peel it apart to use the funnel system for female pilots. I had a tailor make the modifications and tested it at home. We used the same idea for the rubber suit, adding a waterproof zipper around the inseam. Our Life Support group—what the Air Force calls the teams in charge of pilot safety—loved the rubber suit fix and wanted to petition to have the modification be known as the McSally. (I, however, did not want to be known for a pee zipper.)

I didn't need to use the pee zipper on my trip to Kuwait, because I was sent as part of the advance team. But I did conduct a test run of the flight suit's enhanced Velcro system during one of my flights over Iraq. That morning, the sergeant in charge of intelligence stood up to give the pilot briefing and decided to inject some humor into the situation. He talked about our mission: deter Saddam Hussein, identify enemy movement, and the final objective, "Captain McSally is going to take a piss over Iraq." It worked.

WHILE I APPRECIATED MY FLIGHT suit "win," my most treasured victory came slightly earlier. As a brand-new A-10 pilot, just out of training, I won the most difficult bombing competition in my operational squadron, an archaic, World War II-era manual attack style known as "standby pipper." In standby pipper, a pilot could not use modern bombing computers or other high-tech instruments. The only way to deliver your weapons accurately was via a combination of rapid math calculations (trigonometry) and precision flying. No one expected the new girl to post better scores than dozens of highly experienced, veteran pilots. It earned me some respect in advance of deploying, but also caused some discomfort with a few of my fellow pilots. Success definitely has the potential to become a double-edged sword.

In 1997, I was selected to be a full-time A-10 instructor pilot, becoming the first woman to achieve that role. I also was promoted to the rank of major, two years early. Only a very small percentage of officers were promoted two years early, after being recommended by their wing commanders and independently approved by a promotion board with strict rules on selecting officers with the best records and potential. My promotion riled many pilots in the A-10 community, most of whom I didn't know and had never served with. Indeed, the difficulty some pilots had with accepting women seemed to become more pronounced with each promotion.

Fighter pilot squadrons of that era were notorious for keeping a book in which pilots made fun of each other; they were often known as "Hog Logs." What was written ranged from adolescent teasing to notations of flying mistakes to a variety of sexual slurs. Each squadron had one. After they were banned at my base, Davis-Monthan, a Hog Log was still kept in the control tower, a location only accessible to experienced A-10 pilots and instructor pilots. When I did my tours in the tower, I read the disparaging entries about me by guys who weren't even in my squadron. Eventually, the paper book moved online and required log-ins and passwords. Rather than one book for one base, pilots could now sign in from bases all over the world and post comments. Even though I was an A-10 pilot, I was not given access to the online Hog Log, nor did I want it.

(A few years later, one of my A-10 pilot friends printed out a selection of the hostile and raunchy online posts about me so that I could read them. In more than one long comment thread, which featured posts by pilots stationed around the globe from Alaska to South Korea, Germany, and in the continental U.S., my photo was manipulated and accompanied by lines saying, "that f'ing c**t" and "that c**t is no good." A few colonels had even participated in this nonsense, including a commander at the Air Force's much-revered A-10 Weapons School.)

In addition to the write-ups in the Hog Log, I was mocked in other ways. Men at the base taped up denigrating photos and comments about me in their bathrooms. I also received anonymous hate mail and prank calls.

One day, I returned home to a blinking light on my answering machine. The message was a long, ugly diatribe from the wife of an A-10 pilot. She had left a monologue, starting with how I didn't deserve to be a fighter pilot, or an instructor pilot, and definitely did not deserve an early promotion. She continued, saying that I must have slept my way to the top and that the only reason I was being elevated was because I was a woman. She stated that her husband

and other, more experienced A-10 pilots should have been promoted instead. She finished by asking how I could live with myself and look myself in the mirror after being given such an easy road with unearned rewards.

The next morning, I walked into my commander's office with the answering machine in tow and hit play. He listened to the entire rant. Then I left the machine on his desk and told him this was no longer my problem, it was his problem. I said I was going home. When he cleaned up the climate and created a professional environment for me to serve, he should give me a call and I would come back. Then I kept my word; I walked out and drove home.

To his credit, my commander was appalled. Generally, he was aware of the type of crap I dealt with, but to hear the hate from a pilot's wife made it personal and real. He took the tape to his superior, the group commander in charge of every pilot squadron, and the commander took action. Training flights were canceled, and all the A-10 pilots, except for me, were ordered to report to a meeting. As the room stood at attention for the commander's arrival, he walked to the front and played the vicious message. Apparently, one pilot immediately recognized his wife's voice and was horrified. The group commander gave a passionate speech about honor, character, and professionalism. What it means to be a team. Why we put on the uniform. How disgusted he was with the behaviors people had exhibited against another teammate who had been selected through a highly regulated process to move up to the next rank. How we should be celebrating and spurred on to greater excellence, instead of tearing that pilot down, conducting cowardly personal attacks, and having wives leave hateful, anonymous messages. He said he would not tolerate this behavior.

I returned to work the next day. In a twenty-four-hour span, the environment had shifted. I felt like I was no longer fighting alone, and I had learned a valuable lesson. I might be the one being attacked, but it wasn't up to only me to stop it. There was a chain of command responsible for the mission, the people, and the "good order and discipline" of the team. Now that I have been a commander, I know a leader is responsible for setting the vision, the standards, the priorities, and the climate. Two identical units can function completely differently in professionalism, morale, and mission readiness, simply based on their leader.

Our squadron's weapons officer was a good friend of mine. We had already served together for two and a half years in my previous A-10 squadron, had deployed together twice, and he knew me as a friend, fellow pilot, and officer. The day after the pilot meeting, my friend requested to speak with me privately.

Standing in a briefing room, he asked me to forgive him. I said, "For what?" He said he knew firsthand that I was a good pilot and officer. But when he heard the defamatory statements and attacks against me, he had remained silent. He thought he was doing the right thing by keeping his mouth shut and not feeding the frenzy. But now he realized he was being cowardly, afraid to counter the lies spread by people who didn't know me and had never flown with me. He told me he would never stay silent again. I learned a lesson that day about how easily good people can become bystanders and even followers when confronted with strong social pressure. I was grateful my friend recognized this and decided to change. Real courage is shown when a bystander decides to step up and refuses to tolerate behavior that he or she knows is wrong. He kept his word for the rest of his career.

BUT WHILE THE CLIMATE IMPROVED in my assigned squadron, it was more difficult to change the larger Air Force fighter/attack pilot culture. One holdout was the Air Force's elite A-10 Weapons School. Weapons School is the Air Force's equivalent of *Top Gun*, and I am grateful for all those with whom I served who chose to become tactics and weapons experts. Our successful missions relied upon their unique training and expertise, and they were top-notch pilots.

But that didn't mean there weren't a few jerks in Weapons School. Soon after I became an A-10 pilot, several friends told me about a new rule: my name—McSally—couldn't be mentioned in the weapons school bar—and if anyone did, he had to buy a round of drinks for everyone. The rule stipulated that if my name was said, another officer would yell "Ka-Ching," like the sound of an old cash register, indicating the rule-breaker had to pay up. Soon, weapons officers started calling me "McChing" in order to refer to me without having to buy a round of shots or beer. (In the Hog Logs, I later saw that posters wrote "Ka F***ing Ching!!! You said the M-Word.")

I almost found the whole thing hard to believe and didn't let it bother me. But then a friend and squadron mate of mine invited me to attend his black-tie graduation ceremony from Weapons School. He could pick four pilots to fly in for the celebration, and I was honored to be asked. The ceremony, which included graduates from other fighter weapons schools, was held at a casino in downtown Las Vegas. My buddy knew inviting me would cause a ruckus, but he also felt it would send a "statement." He wanted me there.

Before the main event in the massive casino ballroom, each aircraft division held a separate reception. The A-10 Weapons School commander highlighted the graduates' accomplishments and asked them to introduce their guests. When it was my friend's turn, he introduced his family, his vice wing commander, and then his fellow pilot guests. After he said my name, all the Weapons School instructors yelled out in unison, "Ka-Ching!" Pockets of the room erupted in laughter. It was humiliating. Even though there were multiple colonels and commanders standing there who understood exactly what was going on, no one said a word. The program continued as if nothing had happened. My friend who had invited me apologized, and a few of my fellow pilots shook their heads. But I was angry.

I went into dinner and kept replaying the "Ka-Ching" tape in my mind. As the evening ended and people got up to leave, I saw the A-10 Weapons School commander standing off to the side, chatting. Before thinking through the ramifications and bolstered by the "courage" of a couple of beers, I aggressively confronted him, telling him that he should be ashamed of himself and telling him where to get off, not using G-rated words. The three pilots from my squadron raced over and pulled me away, but I felt fantastic. I didn't care that I was a major and he was a lieutenant colonel squadron commander. He deserved it.

When I arrived at work on Monday morning, my squadron commander called me into his office. He had already heard from the A-10 Weapons School commander. That evening, and my tirade, was the first time we had met. It is easy to encourage and tolerate hostility and denigration toward a person you do not know. It is a bit harder to stand face-to-face with the person and be confronted with the truth of the unprofessional behavior you have permitted, and even egged on. The commander felt badly. But he never said anything. Instead, his apology came in the form of ensuring that I was not reprimanded for my own unprofessional behavior. But institutionally nothing really changed. The A-10 Weapons School continued with the "Ka-Ching" practice when my name came up for many years after that.

In 2016, more than twenty-five years after women were allowed to become fighter pilots, a female A-10 pilot did finally graduate from A-10 Weapons School. And I'm certain that when her name was called, no one said "Ka-Ching."

I'm sure as you read this, you're wondering if I ever

thought about quitting the Air Force. The answer is yes. A number of times. But in the end, what was far more powerful was serving, flying, and fighting for my country. The hardest part was knowing that the people who were often the most opposed to me were my teammates. As pilots, we are taught to support each other: In the air, each pilot watches for threats against the others at all times. We know our lives truly are in our squadron mates' hands. The same with our troops on the ground. In combat flying, possibly the worst tragedy is friendly fire, when you shoot at your own forces.

So, it was devastating to face "friendly fire" from the pilots whose backs I was supposed to have—and who were supposed to have mine. This culture wasn't denigrating only to women. Male pilots were also routinely ostracized from the larger pilot pack. It was awful to watch this pack mentality marginalize one person and deny him or her the chance to achieve their destiny or compel them to change who they really are simply to fit in.

I often get asked now what parts of military training and service might have prepared me for the rough world of politics, and I usually say it was figuring out how to have thick skin, so you don't take personal attacks so personally. But also to strike a balance so you never lose your humanity or your sense of humor. This wasn't an easy or quick skill to learn, but I realized when I left at the end of the day, still reeling from some nasty comment, the jerk who said it wasn't giving me a second thought, so why should I ruin my evening thinking about him?

But as difficult as these years sometimes were, I was able to tolerate them because to me the Air Force was never just a job. It was a calling to serve. I love the Air Force and am so grateful for all the amazing opportunities I had while in uniform, including everything from my education to the chance to become an A-10 pilot and command an A-10 squadron. It remains the highest honor of my life to have led men and women in combat and it is the highest privilege to know that our missions helped save lives in the air and on the ground. Each and every day, I served with extraordinary patriots and professionals who sacrificed so much to defend our freedoms. One of my most memorable Christmas Eves was a freezing cold night spent in Afghanistan. I walked on the flight line to encourage our maintenance team responsible for keeping our jets flying. One A-10 had an elusive engine problem and I stayed for a while with the crew chief and engine specialists who were determined to troubleshoot it and fix the plane. Their selfless commitment to our mission, like all the unsung heroes of our armed forces, inspired me and still does. I love our Air Force, and its core values have become my own. Yes, there were places where I hit bumpy skies and turbulence, but I have absolutely no regrets and would do it all again.

The overwhelming majority of combat pilots are people with honor, integrity, and respect; they are extraordinary professionals who love their country and want to serve and fight for it. Sometimes a few jerks can create a toxic climate, which persists when good people go along or say nothing. But this problem exists in many other professions from healthcare to journalism to high-tech, not just inside the military. Countless women and men have walked in my shoes.

These pockets of hostility also do not define all the exceptional officers and pilots I served with, many of whom I consider to be like brothers. And they don't define our Air Force, where I was proud to give my all for twenty-six years.

Even the A-10 Weapons School changed. Eventually people tend to grow up. Nearly all of the A-10 Weapons School guys who were ringleaders or joined in came around to the realization they were wrong. Some even sought me out to apologize. I became close with one of them, and we even dated after we were both retired. We remain friends, and he gave me thoughtful advice on this book, for which I am very grateful. Talk about reconciliation!

FOUR

Mastering the Art of Chair Flying

"The best training isn't just plan, plan, plan, and prepare, prepare, prepare. Sometimes training involves learning how to override our most basic instincts and strongest feelings."

MY PERSONAL PHILOSOPHY FOR SUCCESS in a nutshell? Plan and train harder and better than the competition— whether that competition is swimming next to you in the first leg of a triathlon or trying to shoot you down in combat. If you are truly prepared, you will not only be ready for whatever challenge is in front of you, but also for any contingency that you do not expect.

I was a competitive javelin thrower at the Air Force Academy when my right hand was broken during my senior year. Rather than give up my spot on the team, I decided to learn to throw with my left hand, an idea that seemed ridiculous to my coach and everyone else except me. No surprise, the more they said I couldn't do it, the more determined I was to prove them wrong. My right arm was very much my "good" arm, I was extremely uncoordinated, with limited strength, in my left. I requested to spend one of my classes conducting an independent study, evaluating how to retrain my brain and body to throw lefty (I also had to learn how to write lefty to complete my academics).

For the first few months, I visited the indoor track and heaved a weighted ball into a tarp hundreds of times each day. I developed a new respect for stroke victims and those with brain injuries, who struggle to relearn how to do physical tasks. It was boring, repetitive, and frustrating. The coach and my indoor track teammates mocked me for my silly quest, but I kept throwing that ball. A javelin coach at the U.S. Olympic Training Center in Colorado offered to help me. When outdoor track-and-field season arrived, I had honed my left-handed javelin throw by sheer willpower and repetition. I could not get it to sail quite as far with my left arm as I could with my right, but it was far enough to earn me a spot on the team my senior year. I achieved my goal by having a plan and doing the preparation and work. Although I didn't recognize it at the time, learning to throw lefty—something I never wanted to do—was also excellent preparation for pilot training.

Every A-10 flight begins with the same ritual: the pilot fastens a parachute harness to his or her legs and chest and climbs a ladder to reach the cockpit. Then the crew chief helps the pilot strap into the ejection seat, which contains a survival kit and a raft. Finally, the pilot's antigravity suit, main and emergency oxygen hoses, and a communications cord are connected, and the pilot dons a personalized helmet that has been molded to fit his or her head. Much of this ritual is centered around preparing for one thing that, as an accomplished or novice pilot, you hope never to do: eject.

If something went wrong while I was in the air, I knew to assume a good body position. Then I was trained to pull the ejection handles next to my thighs. Within a fraction of a second, the clear canopy above my head would be blasted from the aircraft and rocket motors located under my seat would fire, shooting me away from the airplane at a force of at least fifteen times the force of gravity (hence the need to get into a good body position to avoid breaking your back, neck, legs, or arms). Depending on my altitude and airspeed, I would either descend in free fall, still strapped to the ejection seat, until I reached a safe height for my parachute to deploy or I would be rapidly separated from the heavy metal seat, with only my survival kit still attached, as my parachute burst open.

In addition to mastering the art of ejection, every pilot needs to be prepared for what could happen next. We undergo intense survival training to prepare for landing in enemy territory. I've been dragged across dry, dusty desert ground by a pickup truck, bumping on divots and being bruised by stray rocks, to simulate high winds dragging my parachute. I've sucked water into my lungs as I've tried to flip onto my back and extricate myself from my parachute while being dragged behind a motorboat. I've been dropped into the wilderness with no food and no water and had to build a shelter, find food, and try to navigate my way to safety, while being hunted by "enemy" forces. I've been "captured" in a classroom, blindfolded, and turned into a POW, locked alone in a tiny cell, except when I was dragged out for interrogation. And so have my fellow military pilots and others at risk of capture.

I wasn't planning to eject on any of my A-10 flights. But neither is any pilot. Every time you step into the aircraft, you need to be equipped, prepared, and mentally ready to make that decision in a split second.

But the best training isn't just plan, plan, plan, and pre-pare, prepare, prepare. Sometimes training involves learning how to override our most basic instincts and strongest feelings.

God definitely did not create human beings to fly. Our "hard wiring" often leads us to think we are flying straight when we are in fact pointed down and vice versa. If you are flying inside clouds, the only way to keep the plane upright is to watch your instruments. I have been in thick clouds, fly-ing straight and level, but my brain and body were convinced that I was rapidly spiraling toward the earth. It feels horrible and requires significant mental energy to ignore your brain and follow only what your instruments tell you. Although I am a proponent of "trust your gut," in a high-stakes situation where emotions can be strong and contradictory, the adage to "trust your instruments," and rely on facts and data, may be more likely to keep you safe—and alive.

There are three types of spatial disorientation. Type 1 is when you are unaware and therefore do nothing to fix it. (Pilots say this is where you "die comfortably.") Type 2 is when you are aware that you are disoriented but can fight it and prevail. Type 3 is when you are so disoriented it is debilitating, and you cannot save yourself. Many pilots die from types 1 and 3. I often use Type 1 as an analogy for life situations where a relationship, a job, or some other factor is spiraling downward but the person does not recognize it. They are comfortable until they "crash." I try to live my life avoiding Type 1.

Imagine these risks, now imagine them spread and multiplied across four to seven planes. When planes fly in close formation, their wingtips are only three feet apart. This "fingertip" formation was how I flew much of the way across the Atlantic for a deployment to the Middle East. We took off from the East Coast and hit bad weather. I was flying three feet away from my flight lead when I saw a lightning bolt hit his plane. The electrical charge entered through the front, traveled the length of the plane, and shattered the light on the plane's tail as it exited.

But as risky as fingertip formation is, it is not as nerve-racking as midair refueling. I always wondered who came up with the idea to refuel airplanes while flying—did they think it was a great idea to have it occur in pitch-black darkness, or inside thick clouds with extremely limited visibility and turbulence, or both? When your car needs fuel, you pull into the gas station, put the car in park, turn off the engine, step out, and place the gas nozzle into your tank. Hardly a white-knuckle experience requiring all of your brain power and concentration. Air refueling, however, consists of one airplane purposely running into another airplane in a mini, controlled collision while traveling around 250 to 300 miles an hour. After the planes connect with each other, highly flammable gas flows from one plane to the other, while they continue flying.

Don't get me wrong—air refueling is a brilliant invention. It allows small, tactical planes like the A-10 to fly across the Atlantic Ocean or across the country without having to land. It enables fighters and other airplanes on combat missions to immediately return to the fight. It allows us to use the planes we have more efficiently.

We call the massive planes filled with fuel "tankers." Each tanker follows a designated rendezvous track and it is up to the pilot whose aircraft needs gas to locate the closest "flying gas station." The tanker is equipped with a window at the rear where the boom operator lies down and lowers a long metal boom with its own little wings. Fuel is dispensed through the boom to the A-10 at about a forty-five-degree angle. But to get that fuel, an A-10 pilot must carefully maneuver—basically fly into—the boom.

Because the A-10's air refueling receptacle is on the plane's nose, the pilot sees the entire process as it happens. For many pilots, including me, there can be a natural flinching reaction as the massive boom lunges toward your plane, which is already moving about 275 miles per hour. Booms have smashed A-10 windscreens. It's very counterintuitive to fly into one. I have completed refueling and been exhausted due to the mental and physical energy required to control the plane and concentrate. I will be eternally thankful to the expert boom operators who, in horrendous weather conditions, confidently and expertly pushed the boom forward to grab my plane as everything bounced around.

Once, when I was a young A-10 pilot flying across the Atlantic in bad weather, I became separated from my group as we waited our turns for refueling. The clouds were thick, and if you lose sight of the tanker or the plane you are flying next to while in close formation, you need to maneuver away to avoid a midair collision. Back then, the A-10 didn't have a GPS, and in the middle of the ocean, there was no capability to radio to land-based air traffic controllers. All we had were a few archaic tools to try to find each other; one tool could tell you how far away you were from another plane but not that other plane's direction relative to you.

After ensuring that I would not have a midair collision, I started searching for the tanker and my group. Our tool showed I was only one mile away. My plane and the tanker group were both flying on the same heading, but I was five hundred feet lower. I increased my airspeed to catch up. The display showed I was flying faster than they were, but the distance between us was barely changing. It didn't make sense. I added more power and suddenly the distance started to increase. I was traveling faster, we were on same heading, how could I be falling further behind?

I tried not to think about being by myself, in thick clouds, over the Atlantic. By the grace of God, I hit a small break in the clouds. That's when the tanker pilots spotted me— flying *in front* of them. It turned out that I had flown a wide circle and passed them. I quickly rejoined the formation and exhaled with relief.

TRAINING IS ALSO OFTEN BEST accomplished in small steps. For three weeks before my first A-10 flight, I underwent intense training on the ground, including a visualization exercise known as chair flying, which is just what it sounds like. I would sit in a kitchen chair in my house, strap my flight checklist to my leg, and mentally rehearse every routine procedure. We used this technique in initial pilot training, too. The idea of chair flying was to make basic elements, such as takeoffs, radio calls, and landing approaches, feel like second nature when I was in the air.

Even when it comes to things that I do for fun, I learn best when I break a new skill into small steps. When I was stationed in the German Alps, I watched paragliders soar over the mountains and decided that I too wanted to fly like a bird. I enrolled in an intensive training program in German, a language I don't speak. (I think the instructor who welcomed me into his class probably gave me too much extra credit for being a military pilot!)

We began with short glides on a training hill. We leapt ten feet off the ground, so any mistakes were unlikely to cause serious injury. When the instructor cleared us for higher flights, he was confident in our skills, and we felt confident, too. Even as a well-trained pilot, had I not been desensitized on that low hill, I never could have progressed to running off the highest mountain in Germany and gliding five thousand feet in the air, over a beautiful lake, listening to nothing but the wind—where I truly understood the meaning of "breathtaking."

Building up to, visualizing, and then repeating a task can help set us up for success and help anyone realize their worries are smaller than they imagined. We discover that disaster may not be lurking around the corner. Instead, we find our confidence.

After I had accumulated enough experience flying the A-10, I could approach takeoff with confidence. The same became true of complex missions, flying in difficult weather conditions, and even midair refueling. I stopped worrying about ejecting; instead, I was grateful to have the training that could save my life.

And that's a pretty good outlook no matter whether you are in the air or have both feet on the ground.

FIVE

Do Things Afraid

"None of us is born either courageous or fearful."

A FEW SUMMERS AFTER MY dad died, I decided to work rather than hang out on the beach in Rhode Island. I found a job as a busgirl at a popular restaurant on the water, which offered an early breakfast for fishermen and other workers heading out before sunrise. I was assigned to the morning shift that started before dawn.

I was excited for my first "real" job beyond babysitting, shoveling snow, or mowing lawns, but I needed to figure out how to get to and from work each morning. It was a long bike ride in the dark, and I didn't want to burden my mother with dropping me off and picking me up. Our house sat on a small pond that connected to the waterfront and ultimately the ocean through a tight passageway under a bridge. I decided to use our family dinghy outfitted with a tiny outboard motor. My dad had taught me how to operate the boat as well as overall water safety. Plus I was a great swimmer, so my mom agreed. I also persuaded my employer to offer me a free boat slip.

The journey was mostly free of hazards, except for that one section beneath the low, narrow bridge. The perfect path was straight through the center, avoiding the rocks and shallow water to the sides. But when the ocean tide flowed in or out, water rushed through the narrow passageway. If the tide was coming in, you could sometimes barely

move; the rushing water pushed against you like a turbulent headwind. In this case, you needed to patiently steer the
little boat without overcorrecting to avoid the sharp rocks.
When the tide raced out, you were swept up in a massive
flow that pushed you rapidly through the passageway from
behind and made the boat sit up high in the water. High tide
required quick thinking and steering to avoid hitting the
top and sides of the bridge, while also ducking your head
so you didn't knock yourself unconscious. There was very
little room for error. When I was growing up, my dad had
taught me how to drive the boat through this passageway
during the tides, but I was still anxious. And I had never
done it solo.

On my first day, I woke before 5:00 A.M. It was dark and
chilly. Even though I had completed a practice run with my
brother, I almost returned to the house and declared that
I had changed my mind. But I didn't. I chose to trust my
training, and the promise I had made to my employer to be
on time. I chose to "pilot the boat afraid." The experience
seems small, but it set a pattern for me to push past other
fears in the future.

Four years later, after I graduated high school, I needed
to find the courage to board an airplane by myself, fly to
Colorado, and start basic training at the Air Force Academy. Transitioning out of high school to the next chapter is
filled with uncertainty, no matter the path. I had accepted
an appointment to the Air Force Academy, but the weeks
between that decision and my plane ride were an emotional

roller coaster. I questioned if I had made the right decision. I regretted leaving my friends, although the reality is that there is no such thing as thirteenth grade—for anyone. You can't go back, you can't cling to a season that has passed, and you can't go forward and replicate it. You have to chart your own path.

I bought some combat boots and was a humorous sight, running around my neighborhood in shorts and tall, lace-up boots to break them in. As my departure day approached, I also cut my hair extremely short—I wanted to do it myself instead of leaving it up to the Air Force's assembly-line cutting system. And I did it to make sure I got on that airplane. There was no way I was going to hang around town with that super-short, quasi-buzz-cut hairstyle.

Besides the combat boots, the only other items they told us to bring with us were bras; they didn't want to try to size and issue them to us. Moving on from high school is stressful, as is moving out of the house and across the country. Added to all that was the fact that when I got off the plane, I was going to be yelled at, because that is how cadets are welcomed to the first day of basic training. The potential for me to be paralyzed by anxiety was real.

But my choice to navigate that boat solo at fourteen helped equip me to board that plane alone at eighteen, which helped me climb into the cockpit of a single-seat A-10 at twenty-eight. Each time, I chose to do things afraid. In fact, what these and many other moments have taught me is that I must do things afraid.

None of us is born either courageous or fearful. We learn courage or fear from patterns—and we can unlearn them as well. It doesn't mean that we will vanquish fear, but it does mean that each of us can find the ability to decide to do things afraid. If our ancestors had waited until they were "unafraid" to leave their caves, the human race might have starved to death waiting to feel secure and safe. Doing things afraid means learning to push through the fear and anxiety, to find a way to the other side.

For most of us, doing things afraid is not an easy strategy to embrace. Courage isn't instilled in people magically or genetically. It is an intentional, deliberate process of learning how to confront fear, then moving forward in spite of it. In choosing to do things afraid, you learn that you have the power to overcome. This gives you confidence to do things afraid the next time. Like an athlete who trains his or her muscles to create muscle memory, you can build courage memory. You can become conditioned not to let fear or anxiety form artificial obstacles that stop you from reaching your goals. As an athlete, your first run is not comfortable or fast, the first ball you throw is not a strike. But you have to start somewhere, by jogging around the block or playing catch in the backyard.

The opposite, however, is also true. If you choose to allow fear to have power over you, you will not push through it. You may have a temporary sense of safety, of having avoided what you feared. But the next time you encounter that same fear, your muscle memory will choose to avoid it, instead of doing things afraid.

Doing things afraid also doesn't mean being reckless. At fourteen, I knew how to pilot that rowboat. At twenty-eight, I didn't just walk onto a military base, hop in an A-10, and taxi to the end of the runway. I had been through extraordinary amounts of training. I had experience in other aircraft, I had passed all the tests, and my instructors and commanders had total trust that I was equipped to fly that multimillion-dollar plane. On the day when I started the engines for my flight, I stopped at the end of the runway arming area, where the crew performed final safety checks. After the last check, the ground crew leader told me everything looked good and to "Have a safe flight, ma'am." That was the final piece of encouragement (which means to put courage in another!) that I needed to push through my fear and take off.

WHAT I WILL ALSO NEVER forget from that first flight or any other flight is that no one takes off alone. Pilots receive the majority of the attention and the accolades, but none of us would be in the sky without the people who support us on the ground. While we sit in climate-controlled cockpits, a team of amazing airmen crew chiefs are stationed outside, from sub-zero Alaska or South Korea to blazing hot Arizona or the Middle East, dedicating themselves to keeping

Air Force aircraft flying and pilots safe. It takes a veritable army of specialists in all tasks on the ground around the world to keep our A-10s flying, something that we never forget.

The A-10 Warthog is a gritty airplane, and it requires grit to fly. It is designed to provide "close air support." Built around a powerful 30mm gun, it can carry bombs, missiles, rockets, and up to 1,174 rounds of bullets, the largest such arsenal of any fighter or attack aircraft in the world. It was also built to survive direct hits on the front lines. The cockpit is surrounded by titanium (we call it a titanium bathtub) to prevent bullets from penetrating. An A-10 can be shot up to the point where it loses an engine, all hydraulics, all electronics, and is riddled with holes, and the pilot can still fly it to safety. While the A-10 is lumped into a broad category of aircraft assignments called fighters, our community defines the A-10 as an attack plane, not a fighter. Hence the letter A before the number 10. We are basically the only ones who call it an attack plane, and our group battle cry is "Attack!," which is even how we often sign off on emails. I know my A-10 buddies will bristle to read the A-10 being called a fighter, so I just want to clarify that the plane is uniquely suited for air-to-ground attack missions against enemy ground forces and is actually an attack plane.

The ultimate goal of all our training in the Warthog was to plan and prepare for every possible contingency, because combat is one big contingency. No matter how well-trained, well-equipped, and ready you are, as a nineteenth-century Prussian commander once said, "No plan survives first contact with the enemy." Combat differs from every other human experience in that you must face people whose primary mission is to kill you. And during war, we do not always know where or when.

In Afghanistan, I commanded the 354th Expeditionary Fighter Squadron. Our mission was to provide 24/7 close air support and lead combat search and rescue efforts if a pilot ejected or ground troops became isolated and needed to be extracted from enemy territory. We also escorted convoys or helicopters through hostile zones, helping deter or respond to ambushes. We protected ground special operations forces from above during raids against insurgents and terrorists. For every flight, we took off carrying maps of the entire country, so we would be prepared if we were suddenly diverted to aid troops under fire. Command and control would provide us with the troops' location, call sign, and radio frequency, but often with no background on the situation. Our instructions were simply: just go there and figure it out.

On September 24, 2005, I was suiting up to lead a combat mission and help familiarize an experienced pilot who was making his first flight inside Afghanistan. As we prepared to take off, we were re-tasked to relieve two A-10s from my squadron that were running low on fuel. They had been called in to assist U. S. special forces who were under fire. We scrambled our Warthogs and headed to southern Afghanistan.

A special forces team had been conducting reconnaissance inside a winding canyon when it encountered a hornet's nest of insurgents. Our troops had been forced to separate into many groups and were running low on both ammunition and water. We had to destroy the insurgents from the air, but because they were so enmeshed with the U.S. forces, the risk of wounding or killing our own troops with friendly fire was high. The departing A-10 pilot told me where to find the target area: I was to search for a particular tree near a curve in the canyon. As soon as I saw it, he peeled away to return to base.

I radioed the Joint Terminal Attack Controller (JTAC) on the ground. These controllers are specially trained to call in air strikes on an enemy that is very close to our forces. Their voice is the lifeline between a pilot overhead and the troops under siege on the ground. We only know each other's call signs, and yet the times I've been on the radio with a JTAC are among the most profound moments I have ever spent with another human being. We are speaking the language of life and death. I never knew what this JTAC thought when he heard a female voice at the other end of the line, or if he even thought about it at all, if he simply trusted my training as I trusted his.

I took down the coordinates and information on the insurgents, as well their distance from our troops, and plotted the locations on my map with a grease pencil. When the JTAC wanted to show me his position, he pulled out a mirror to shine the sun in my eyes so I could see his location, without the enemy spotting him. Sometimes the simple stuff works best.

The gun is generally the weapon of choice in these situations. It's better than a bomb to accurately hit a target with less risk of hurting anyone nearby. But in a winding canyon terrain with good and bad guys mixed together, it is very difficult to only shoot the bad guys; our forces could be inadvertently wounded or killed as well. The Americans were climbing the sides of the canyon, with the militants in close pursuit.

While my wingman covered me, I dove and shot two phosphorous rockets to confirm the target location. The rockets hit the ground and released a large, white plume of smoke, allowing the JTAC, as well as my wingman and me, to have a visual reference. I maneuvered my aircraft up and away, and the JTAC told me the target I needed to hit was even closer to him than where the rockets had landed. Any margin for error was small and shrinking. I came around quickly for a second rocket pass. When the smoke rose, I could hear him on the radio. "Shack," he said, using my call sign, "that's the target, that's the target! Come back in with guns!"

As I maneuvered the plane to set up for a guns pass, I realized that my entire electronic cockpit display (the heads-up display, or HUD) had failed. This was the display that showed all the aircraft's critical flight and navigation information. I used my HUD not only to fly, but also to fire my weapons at just the right moment at precisely the right target. Now, the HUD was gone. I quickly went through my procedures: I turned it off and on a few times, checked for other electrical issues, but it remained blank and dark. For years, pilots had been told that an entire HUD would never fail. Portions of the system might fail or degrade and be less effective, but never the whole display.

My wingman and I were starting to run low on gas, with no A-10s close enough to relieve us. I had to make a choice. Should I shoot the 30mm gun using World War II–era tactics and a World War II–era fixed gunsight? This required me to do some really quick—and really important—math, then I had to position my plane at a steep angle and start my attack at the only correct spot to ensure that I would line up perfectly over the target. I would be pointing my plane's nose and its gun into a tangled mess of friendly troops and enemy insurgents, and open fire.

I didn't hesitate—even if I felt the nauseating fear of failure: the profound risk that my bullets could inadvertently hit our troops.

I flew my aircraft around to set up for the attack. I had flown many times on the Barry Goldwater training range in Arizona preparing for a moment like this—it was also similar to the standby pipper competition I had won as a new pilot. I referenced and memorized the calculations for a thirty-degree guns pass on a board Velcroed to my thigh. I climbed to the correct altitude and airspeed, dialed up my manual gunsight, confirmed the gun was armed, and held up my fist to check that I was flying at the correct altitude and was the right distance away from the target. Then I said the fighter pilots' prayer, "God, please don't let me mess this up."

I pushed the power to max, sent my Warthog into the final attack dive, and called, "One's in hot."

"Cleared hot, One," replied the JTAC. I rolled my plane and had about four seconds to correct my alignment for altitude, airspeed, dive angle, and winds. Diving toward the ground at 354 miles per hour, I began my final attack run, opening fire as my plane screamed toward the canyon. The gun unleashed several hundred rounds before I pulled out of my dive and off the target.

"Shack, One! You got 'em! Good hits! Cleared immediate re-attack." My wingman followed me, and I made a second and third pass before having to depart because of low fuel. Those runs bought the American team valuable time to regroup and hunker down. Other A-10s from my squadron arrived later to provide cover, and the entire special forces team was safely extracted that night. I was awarded an Air Medal for that mission and cited for professional skill, courage, and airmanship. I treasure that medal because I knew that the risk—from friendly or enemy fire—was so high for those brave, trapped Americans. That day, all of us did what we were trained to do, and we succeeded, thanks to our preparation, grit, and no small amount of prayer.

SIX

Don't Hesitate to Call a Knock It Off

"Often the only way we learn is through mistakes—and if we are fortunate, we are able to look back, reevaluate, and see where we went wrong."

THE MOST DREADED PART OF pilot training did not happen in the cockpit. It occurred every morning when one instructor led "stand-up." He or she would recite a scenario leading to an aircraft malfunction or emergency, and then, just as disaster was striking the plane, stop, pick a student, and say, "Lieutenant McSally, you have the aircraft."

I would have to stand at attention and explain how I, as the pilot, would handle the situation—what actions would I take first? What was my analysis of the problem based on the information I had? And what would I do to resolve the emergency and get the aircraft and myself back to base? Any mistake, from an incorrect analysis to a misspoken word to a misapplied checklist, and I would hear an angry instructor yell the dreaded words: "Sit down, Lieutenant McSally," followed by "Lieutenant Smith, you have the aircraft," giving another classmate the opportunity to excel or fail. If you were ordered to sit down, you were grounded from flying that day, earned a failing grade for stand-up, and were sent to remedial training.

We all understood the purpose of stand-up. It trained you how to think, analyze, decide, and act under stress. Standing at attention in front of an entire class is nothing compared to the stress of having two engines flame out or an engine catch fire on takeoff, or suffer a complete hydraulic or electrical failure (or a blank HUD screen on a risky attack run) or be at the controls of an aircraft spinning out of control, inverted toward the ground.

Although I dealt with many emergencies as a pilot, the closest I came to dying in a plane was in training, on the Nellis range in Nevada, not long after I returned from my first deployment to the Middle East. For six months before I deployed, I had learned all the basics of A-10 missions, flying different scenarios at different altitudes, day and night. But when I deployed, all I did, day after day, was higher-altitude, no-fly-zone enforcement above 10,000 feet. I was flying, but not at a mere five hundred feet above the desert. (We eventually "trained down" to one hundred feet, a very low number considering that the A-10's wingspan clocks in at fifty-seven feet!) There was no time for any kind of weekly refresher training, and even an experienced flyer's skills can atrophy. But I was a "newbie."

Soon after we returned home, I was sent on a joint training exercise with Army ground forces at Nellis Air Force Base in Nevada. It was desert and around 120 degrees, and while the A-10 is a great plane, it wasn't built for heat. Its engines become sluggish and can't respond quickly in hot situations. I was also the only new pilot to have joined my squadron in a very long time; everyone else had practiced dropping live bombs at low altitude for years.

That day, a chain of bad elements lined up—an inexperienced pilot, a lapse in low-altitude training, live bombs, an unfamiliar place, and the heat—before I ever left the ground. As we know from most reports on plane crashes, it is usually not one thing that brings down an airplane, it is a cascade of failures.

WE WERE FLYING SCENARIOS FOR high-threat attacks, where there was no opportunity to plan, and I couldn't see the target in advance. We would head toward the target at five hundred feet, about one and a half football fields, above the ground and perform a series of maneuvers, flying to the side, then up to find the exact target, and then upside down. At the end, we had to be flying straight in a dive and we had three to five seconds to make final corrections. At such low altitudes, if a pilot gets distracted during these maneuvers, he or she can fly into the ground in seconds.

My checks and feel for low-altitude flying were months old. We are taught to abort if we aren't maintaining a specific dive angle. That day, my brain synapses were firing a little too slowly, and I didn't realize that I was coming in too steeply as I prepared to drop my bomb. Coming in at the wrong angle can do two things: turn the weapon into a dud or leave you too close to an exploding bomb, which can hit you with blast fragments and possibly blow you up as well. I realized I had messed up as soon as the bomb released. That meant I needed to get away, fast.

My last task was to execute a safe escape. I had to pull

the plane out of the dive, turn it sixty degrees, and speed off. I pulled up and made the turn, but as I did so, I looked over my shoulder to see if the bomb had detonated. In that instant, the nose of my plane was not level, it was slightly low. Which meant that instead of flying to safety, I was now speeding toward the ground, with my eyes focused behind me.

This is how a lot of people die in A-10s—low altitude, no room for error, looking somewhere other than out front. The letters "R.B." flashed across my brain—for R. B. Truesdale, one of my A-10 instructors, who despite being a veteran pilot, died in an exercise almost exactly like this. I looked forward and saw my airplane in a full dive toward the ground and pulled up hard on my stick to recover. I climbed to a safe altitude, and I lived. I still don't know why.

What I should have done next was call a "knock it off" and fly back to base, since I had come close to crashing and dying. As soon as a pilot says, "Knock it off," every pilot in the vicinity knows to stop maneuvering, climb to a safe altitude, and then figure out what happened. Calling a knock it off is designed to ensure that everyone stays safe and everyone goes home. Once you land, you can figure out all the ways you went wrong. But I didn't do that. I shook it off and moved on to the next attack maneuver. Later, in the debriefing room, I said, "Look, I made some mistakes on this run." My flight lead watched the tape and said, "Holy crap. You almost killed yourself today."

The next day, I was back in the saddle training at low altitude.

IN ALL MY YEARS IN the military, every friend I lost in an airplane crash died during training. It is hard to teach this lesson to Type A people, but no matter what the reason, if you are not fully physically and mentally engaged and ready to fly, you shouldn't. Grounded is always better than dead. I didn't fully learn that lesson in 1995 on the Nellis range, instead I learned it in the spring of 1997.

That April, my friend Craig Button, who had been a T-37 instructor pilot in Del Rio with me, disappeared while on an A-10 training mission. I knew he had arrived at my base in Tucson, but we hadn't reconnected. He had called me a while before and left a message, but my life was overwhelmed with work, volunteer activities, a major project at my home, and wedding plans. I had planned to call Craig back, but never got around to it, and now he was missing.

I felt guilty and mad at myself. I channeled that energy into helping with the search and rescue operation. From the radar and pilot reports, it became clear that he had flown his A-10 off course, north to Colorado. People speculated that Craig had purposely flown into a mountain. Although the subsequent investigation did not arrive at any definitive proof, I was tortured by the possibility that his call was an attempt to reach out to a friend during a moment of turmoil, and I had let him down. Back then, it was almost taboo to talk about mental health, let alone suicide, in the military. The Defense Department didn't even start tracking self-inflicted deaths until 2001. The stigma was as bad as the pain. Today, military suicide rates are on par with the increasing and devastating toll suicide takes in civilian life. We've all been touched by it. A loved one who directly experienced this tragedy said something that has stuck with me: "Suicide doesn't end the pain, it just transfers it to those you leave behind." To combat this epidemic, the military services have started several initiatives for early identification and support, but the numbers are still unacceptably high. We, however, had none of that support when Craig was serving.

NEARLY THREE WEEKS AFTER CRAIG disappeared, I was flying in a search helicopter when we spotted what looked like wreckage in the snow on the side of a Colorado mountain. The pilot set one skid down, and I stepped out onto the other skid to grab debris fragments. Slightly above where we were hovering, I saw what looked like Craig's flight checklist. I still foolishly hoped Craig had ejected. Seeing his checklist, I knew that his remains were likely buried in that snow. The next day, para-rescue teams recovered a small portion of his remains. We held a memorial service, and I returned to work.

Back in the cockpit of an A-10 for the first time in more than three weeks, I felt numb and not totally focused. As

I conducted the preflight inspection, I recalled the twisted metal of Craig's A-10, scattered across a snowy mountainside. I pictured the parts of my plane as mangled pieces.

I completed my checklists and began to taxi, but I was merely going through the motions. Have you ever driven to work, as you do every day, and pulled into the parking lot with no recollection of how you got there? Now, I was on the runway, engines revving, with that same feeling. As I waited to be cleared for takeoff, I thought: "Craig taxied out and waited here on April 2 in his own A-10. Two hours later, his body was pulverized as his plane slammed into the side of the mountain." I pictured him sitting where I was and then envisioned his body being crushed against the instrument panel as his A-10 hit the rocks and snow.

The tower told me to go, and I headed to the training range. I flew a roughly two-hour mission and returned safely. But I realized I was distracted and needed to take a few days off. I was sleep-deprived from the search for Craig, and, in addition to the "normal grief" of losing a buddy, I was trying to process the agonizing reality that he might have chosen to die. Anyone who knows someone who took their own life can understand the deep guilt of wondering what we could have done to stop it. I talked to my commander, and he agreed. Pilots need to be 100 percent. I have seen friends and fellow pilots make the right decision not to fly for any number of reasons. As a commander, I have directed someone not to fly because they didn't sleep well the night before, or had a fight with their wife, or a loved one was ill or had passed away.

My flight commander took me off flight duty for the rest of the week. But the next day, a squadron pilot couldn't fly his mission, and the scheduler posted my name on the list. I let my pride and a belief that I could compartmentalize my grief allow me to accept the assignment. Again, I stepped into the jet and visualized each piece as it had looked at Craig's crash site. Again, I imagined Craig's last seconds of life as he sat in a cockpit identical to mine. Again, I went through the motions of the checklist to start, taxi, and takeoff.

We recheck our fuel right after takeoff. I looked at my fuel gauge and reported "2.8" on the radio to my wingman. Wait, I thought, did I just say 2.8? In standard conditions, an A-10 carries about ten thousand pounds of gas. We plan to end our missions at what is called "bingo" fuel, so we can land with about fifteen hundred pounds of gas. (Twelve hundred pounds is "minimum" fuel; eight hundred pounds is an emergency.) I read the gauge again, and it said twenty-eight hundred pounds. I tested the gauge and told my wingman we were returning to base. It turned out that the crew chief had forgotten to coordinate refueling the aircraft. Yet somehow, it was signed off and sent to fly again.

But the final failure was mine. A central part of the pilot checklist before leaving the ground is to check the fuel level and test the fuel gauge. I am sure I looked at it and tested it, but I clearly wasn't paying complete attention. I never experienced this type of failure before or since, but it was truly a blessing: low fuel kept me from conducting a training mission when I should have been on the ground.

After a few days off, I was back in the air, still juggling a lot but ready to focus and compartmentalize. On May 27, I was scheduled to lead three planes on a nighttime training run to the northern tactical (NorthTac) segment of the bombing range. The mission included an air refueling. I remember it being a dark night with no moon. It was impossible to see the horizon with the naked eye or even with night-vision goggles (NVGs).

We had just started using NVGs. The lighting in the cockpits was not compatible with the goggles, so we had to jury-rig our instrument panels, Velcroing translucent filters over the instrument gauges and placing electrical tape around any spaces where white light showed. Looking back, it was a little ridiculous and very unsafe. The Air Force could have invested in modifying the lighting in the A-10 to be compatible with the goggles. Instead, we got a half-baked solution, which required a lot of time and effort—we had to spend significant extra time in the cockpit making these modifications before each night flight—and it still wasn't right.

The filters made it hard to see the instruments, but if we increased the lights, we couldn't see clearly outside of the cockpit. To compensate, most pilots also flew with little lights Velcroed around their index fingers, to be able to see the instruments and gauges in a crunch. (Velcro was definitely invaluable to pilots in the 1990s and beyond.)

Another training mission was also scheduled that night, with another A-10 fighter pilot, Captain Amy Svoboda. Their group was headed to SouthTac, the southern tactical range, located adjacent to the area where my group was flying. Amy had graduated from the Air Force Academy a year after me. But until she joined my squadron, I didn't really know her. I was the only woman in the unit, and I was a little ambivalent about her arrival.

In a male-dominated environment like the military, it would seem logical that women would stick together and support each other. I am not a sociologist, but in my experience, the opposite happened. It was often every woman for herself, and the women were harsher on each other than on their male counterparts. We operated in a high-stress, high-stakes environment. Most female pilots were very much Type A people, who would rather control the outcome by excelling and being judged on their performance. It wasn't uncommon for some female pilots (or cadets at the academy) to adopt the attitude of "I'm one of the guys and you're not," preemptively isolating any new female squadron mate.

I wasn't sure what to think about Amy until I met her in 1996. She was skilled, professional, and very likable, and she quickly earned the respect of the squadron team. Much of the hostility I had experienced when transitioning into fighters two years before had fortunately subsided. Amy was accepted like any other pilot, and I soon realized it was awesome to have a wingwoman around! Together, Amy and I were a stronger force against typical fighter pilot banter and teasing. Amy also seemed to find the perfect balance between being a fighter pilot and a woman, something I struggled with as I tried to fit in. Amy brightened up a room with her smile, her attitude, and her wit—and she was a great pilot and officer, too.

AT ONE POINT DURING OUR night mission, I directed my group of three pilots to attack our next target. One of my wingmen was highly experienced and a Weapons School graduate. It was so dark and disorienting outside our windows that he responded, "Hang on, it is so dark out here, it is taking nearly all my brain cells to just fly my airplane and stay on the range."

Soon after, I saw a major fire burning on the ground to the south. I was confused at first. A training bomb or rocket or flare can start a small ground fire, but this was huge. A few seconds later, I heard the emergency call: an aircraft on SouthTac had crashed. Oh, God, I thought. *No!*

I waited on the radio to hear who had crashed. It was Amy.

During the day, it would be easy to see if the pilot had ejected, but it was much more difficult at night, even with night vision and especially on a night like this. While Amy's flight lead refueled, I took over as on-scene commander. We searched for any signs of movement on the ground. I called over and over again on the radio to Amy, in case she had ejected, but there was only silence.

When our planes reached "bingo fuel," we had to fly home. It was a long, quiet return to the base. A ground crew would head to the crash site at dawn. I know now that this meant that the base commander believed Amy was dead. I went home and sat on my couch in shock, unable to sleep, praying that Amy would somehow be found alive.

That morning, I was scheduled to sing the national anthem at the base's annual Memorial Day ceremony. I sang it with my whole heart. The 21-gun salute and the lone bugler playing taps brought me to the verge of tears.

After the ceremony, there was a small reception. As I stood in the coffee line, another pilot said, "I wanted you to know I am really sorry about the loss of your friend." I looked at him and numbly answered, "Which one?" He was taken aback. He was talking about Craig, but I wasn't sure if he was referring to Amy. I was the only person on base who was friends with them both.

Her death was confirmed a short while later. The whole squadron was devastated. Amy had been slated to deploy to the Middle East in a matter of weeks. Instead, we held a beautiful memorial service for her. I had the privilege to speak about what an inspiration she was to me. She was buried at a cemetery on the grounds of the Air Force Academy on June 12, 1997. I flew as the "missing woman" in the traditional missing man formation, a special maneuver performed at military funerals.

Four planes take off and wait away from the ceremony. Before the flyover, we maneuver into close formation, each plane's wingtip just three feet apart from the next aircraft's. The flight lead has one plane on his left wing, and two planes on his right wing. When we are overhead, the lead directs the plane closest to him on the right to pull up and away from the formation, creating a gap to honor the pilot we have lost. It was the most devastating honor I ever performed.

NO MATTER HOW MANY YEARS pass, I will never understand why R.B., Craig, and Amy died, but I lived.

Every pilot makes mistakes. There is no way to be mistake-free in any profession. There is also no way to eliminate risk. For pilots, our mistakes and our risks have higher consequences than many because they can get us killed. But often the only way we learn is through mistakes—and if we are fortunate, we are able to look back, reevaluate, and see where we went wrong. We also have to be willing to be honest with ourselves—to admit to and learn from unwanted circumstances and also failures. There's no need to fear mistakes, but certainly we need to prepare for them to happen. And to understand that we all have limits. Pilots should never fear changing course or calling a "knock it off."

THE MORNING BEFORE AMY DIED, I called the base chaplain and asked for an appointment. I wanted to talk through Craig's death and also a major life choice. In a few weeks,

I was getting married to a fellow officer. Unlike some pilots, he was professional and kind, and had welcomed me
as a new member of the team. He was a person of faith, and
we developed a close friendship while serving together in
the music ministry at the base chapel. When we were both
deployed to Kuwait, we lifted weights together at the gym,
spotting for each other. I still often do that same weight
workout today. We decided to take our close friendship to
the next level.

I was happy to have found someone who was an encouraging presence, accepting of me, and who loved me as I was.
I had just turned thirty, and many of my friends were married and having children. I thought it was my time as well.
I wanted a husband who would be my partner for life, to
balance me and challenge me; someone I could love and be
loved by; someone I could encourage to be his best, and who
could encourage me to be my best.

We decided to get married in June 1997 (on the same day
as my dad and mom had wed), and many friends agreed it
was a good decision. My fiancé was stationed in South Korea for a year, but would use his leave for the wedding, then
return to serve the last six months of his tour. We planned
an amazing wedding day, which I wanted to be unconventional, and my fiancé supported my ideas. We selected a resort on the north side of Tucson and decided to have the
ceremony outside at sunrise. To time it just right, especially
with a string of jagged mountains, we needed more than the
official sunrise time posted in the local newspaper. A-10 pi-

lots have access to meteorological programs that give the sun azimuth and angle, to assist when we fire Maverick missiles. Consulting these programs, along with a detailed topographical map, a compass, and a protractor, we planned for an exchange of vows at the precise moment when the sunlight would fall upon us. Who knew the Maverick missile program could help with wedding planning?

After a gorgeous dawn ceremony, we and our guests would share a nice breakfast, followed by eighteen holes of golf at the resort. That night, we had planned a fun party—I wanted to avoid the father-bride dance and tossing the bouquet or the garter, which I had always found uncomfortable as a single woman. We rented a pavilion at the park in my neighborhood, hired a DJ and a caterer, and planned a BBQ. Shorts and flip-flops were welcome. People could bring their families and their dogs and just eat, drink, dance, and enjoy. I was excited about this nontraditional, perfect wedding day.

About sixty days before we were to speak our vows, and after Craig died, I started to question whether we should be married. I had a feeling in my gut that I was making a mistake but wasn't sure if my reluctance was due to grief or something else. It seems silly now, but I felt the tremendous pressure of my whole family and my fiancé's family, of all the people who had bought nonrefundable tickets, made hotel reservations, taken time off work, just to attend our wedding. If you're thinking straight, of course, none of this should really matter, but it weighed on me, a lot. I kept doubting my gut instinct and repeating the phrase "the train has already left the station." But it is not a good idea to allow inertia, plane tickets, or others' expectations to be the deciding factors in a life-changing decision.

I had one more chance to talk through my decision: I was supposed to meet with the base chaplain. Then Amy died.

I never rescheduled my appointment. Everyone was focused on honoring Amy and supporting her family. On June 29, family, friends, and squadron mates from Tucson arrived for our Maverick-programmed, perfectly scheduled ceremony. Soon after, my now-husband returned to South Korea. Every relationship faces challenges, but we had some unexpectedly tough challenges from the start. We worked on ours with counseling, periods of separation, and trying to start over, but it became clear that a long, loving marriage wasn't in our future. There wasn't anything wrong with us, it was that we weren't supposed to be married to each other. If I had acted on my original apprehensions, if I had called a knock it off, I would have spared both of us a lot of hurt. Two and a half years later, after a lot of pain and with our hopes and dreams crushed, we parted. Friends who knew us both well said we probably had hung on too long, because neither of us liked to quit at anything, especially when we had taken a vow before God. I know that he did marry again, and I wish only good things for him and his wife. I am still praying for the man God has for me.

The full experience of living life is like a sine wave, a continuous, oscillating wave that moves up and down. On the top are joy, love, peace, intimacy, and acceptance. At the bottom are hurt, disappointment, pain, grief, and anger. If you successfully do whatever it takes to avoid the bottom of the sine wave or harden your heart in response to experiences there, you will also cut off the opportunity to experience the wonderful dynamics of life and deeply enriching relationships at the top. It's not worth it. But in 1997, I spent far too much time at the bottom of the sine wave. I am grateful for all the experiences at the top, but I count that year as the most difficult of my adult life. So far. At one particularly low point, I was talking to another chaplain, who wasn't known for his bedside manner. In a matter-of-fact way, he said, "Martha, sometimes we are all like a jackass in a hailstorm. You just have to sit there and take it and eventually the weather will change." It wasn't what I wanted to hear, and it wasn't delivered with much compassion, but it had raw wisdom. Sometimes we need to grind through a hard season, day by day, hour by hour. The weather will eventually change. And we can help change it with our choices, attitude, and perspective.

SEVEN

Write a Sticky Note or Two

"We need to do our part, but then accept that the final outcome is often beyond our control and place our trust in God."

EVERY DAY WHEN HE WAS in college, my dad's friends would find him kneeling in prayer. I was blessed to grow up in a family of faith, learning about God and Jesus in religious classes and Sunday services, and I accepted it all as the truth. I prayed the rote, expected prayers as a kid, but I never reached out personally to God with petitions, gratitude, or anything else.

Then this loving God took my father from me. Either He was absent, or He was there, and both possibilities seemed disturbing.

I questioned the whole idea of faith, I didn't want to go to church services, and I was deeply angry at this God I knew about but didn't really know.

There is a saying that there are no atheists in foxholes. Those of us who face death so overtly by putting on the uniform and going into harm's way are often pushed to wrestle with what we believe and why, what will happen after we die, and whether God really hears our prayers for courage and safety in the heat of battle. For me, this wrestling started after my dad died, but it accelerated when I headed off to basic training at the Air Force Academy.

Change in geography can be good, but no matter where you run to, you ultimately can't run away from the pain in your life or from internal struggles or lack of peace. On paper at the academy, I was succeeding on all fronts, but my achievements couldn't hide the fact that inside me something was still missing. I longed for something more.

Thankfully, God placed some key people in my path at this critical time. The academy's swim coach was a man of faith and so were many of the upperclassmen on the swim team. I looked to them for advice and followed them to fellowship meetings for nearly a year. I heard friends and other cadets talking about a very real, personal relationship with God. How God met them in their time of need, loved them unconditionally as they were, and sacrificed His son's life so they were forgiven. I wanted what they had, but it took a while for me to truly trust God, cry out to Him, and invite Him into my heart and life as *my* savior, counselor, father, and friend. When I finally surrendered in a service at the cadet chapel in early 1986, during my sophomore year, I felt like a thousand-pound weight had been lifted off my back. For the first time, I sensed true peace and supernatural love from my Creator.

That didn't mean all my problems were solved, pain removed, and patterns changed in an immediate, miraculous way. Finding your own faith also doesn't mean you will be protected from future pain—I certainly wasn't— but it does mean that God is with you and will be with you in the hardest places, leading you through to find joy and peace.

ONE EXAMPLE OF HOW GOD met me in a time of need was after Amy died. While I was working through my grief, I couldn't help but feel anger inside every time I saw the moon. The night she died was so dark, you couldn't tell up from down. But making that flight on a night with a full moon would have changed the dynamic—it might have broken the chain of events that led to her crash.

In my logic of grief, I believed that if the moon had been shining on that fateful night, Amy would be alive. I would stand in my backyard, see the moon, and mutter to myself, "Stupid moon!" I would be driving home from work, see the moon in the night sky, and say, "Stupid moon, where were you when we needed you?" It got to the point where I couldn't see the moon without immediately thinking "stupid moon."

One night in my backyard, I saw the stupid moon and started yelling at it. Why didn't you appear that night? Where were you when we needed you? God's spirit quickly woke me up to the understanding that I wasn't really mad at the moon, I was mad at God for taking Amy. And I was also mad at myself. I was in charge of the squadron's schedule, and I was the one who had scheduled her to fly that awful night.

I fell to my knees in my moonlit backyard and cried out to God, with my anger, disappointment, and feelings of guilt. He met me there with His healing spirit, providing comfort, relief, and peace. It didn't mean my deep grief and feelings of loss were repaired, but it was a moment of genuine healing in that awful year of 1997.

GOD USES MANY WAYS TO get our attention, lead us, prompt us, and speak to us. His ways are mysterious, but His hand of love and leading in my life are very real. In my case, especially because I can be very task-oriented and focused on action, He often grabs my heart through a song. I became involved in leading the worship service music at my base chapel and on deployments as an expression of my faith and a way to ensure that my mind and my heart were open and listening.

I found inspiration in the faith journeys of others as well. I watched as my friend Stacy found her own faith in the middle of the desert, on a combat deployment with our squadron to the Middle East. Neither of us knew how much she would be tested a few years later when she had to fight for her life against leukemia. Her courage, her resilience, optimism, and encouragement of others are contagious and motivational. Her survival is a miracle, and the depth of her faith in the midst of unimaginable challenges remains a shining example to me.

I have also grown and matured in my relationship with God during this lifelong journey. Over time, I have learned not to ignore His promptings to check in with someone or follow up on something. When I sense God is leading me to a difficult or big decision, such as risking my military career to fight for servicewomen or changing paths to run for Congress, I tend to wrestle with the choice for a while before I finally submit. But I eventually do submit and, as I get older, I find that I tend to wrestle less.

I still have my quirky human tendencies of trying to use brute force to make things happen by myself, instead of simply doing my part and trusting that God sees the bigger picture and is in charge of the outcome. Don't get me wrong, as the scripture says, "Faith without works is dead." We need to do our part, but then accept that the final outcome is often beyond our control and place our trust in God. As it is written in Jeremiah 29:11, "I know the plans I have for you," says the Lord. "Plans to prosper you and not harm you. Plans for a hope and a future." The outcome may not be what we wanted, but I would rather have His plans for my life than mine any day.

When my pilot qualification for my height was denied and then my hand was broken, I didn't see God's plan in it. But, had I not been delayed getting my flight clearance, I wouldn't have applied for a scholarship to graduate school at Harvard. Had I not spent two years in graduate school, I wouldn't have started pilot training two years after the rest of my academy class. Had I not been delayed, by the time I graduated from pilot training, the law restricting women from all combat airplanes would have still been in place. Even if I had chosen a T-38 or T-37 assignment to start, by 1993, when the policy finally changed, I would have finished that first assignment and moved on to flying cargo or tanker airplanes—which is exactly what happened to my other female academy classmates. That meant I wouldn't have been allowed to change tracks to move to flying fighters.

So, if I hadn't been too short and hadn't broken my hand, I would have missed the opportunity to become a fighter pilot and fulfill my dreams. As I look back with humility, I realize I don't always see a big picture in the moment. What I consider to be setbacks and barriers instead can be ways for God's hand to move my life on a path that is following His plans. Today, I thank God for my shortness and my broken finger!

In 2012, it was clear to me that God was calling me to quit my current job, return home to Tucson, and run for Congress, with no political experience. I followed the calling and trusted God with the outcome. Just because I was called to run didn't mean I was called to win. He might want me to learn something, or meet someone, or have some other important experience. But I am a warrior, and competitive, and don't like to lose, so I balanced the peace He gave me to trust Him with my drive to do everything I could to achieve victory. After I thought I had won but instead lost fourteen days later, I wasn't angry, but it took me several months to accept that I was being called to run again.

In 2014, toward the end of that second neck-and-neck race, I put two sticky notes on my bathroom mirror. One said HOPE, the other said TRUST. I put them there to remind me every morning of who was truly in charge. I prayed alone and with others for courage, favor, and protection.

Together, we prayed the voters would see me for who I really am, not as the caricature of how I was being portrayed by my opponent's and interest groups' attack ads. A few days after Election Day, it appeared history was going to repeat itself, and I would be facing the same outcome as I did in 2012. As more ballots were counted, it looked as if I was on track to lose by a couple of hundred votes.

I was mad. After more than three long, hard years, was I really going to lose by less than .01 percent? I went out for a run in the desert and yelled at God. My rant went something like this: "God, what's the deal? I thought I was called to serve in Congress. It has been a hard, three-year battle. Fine! I will go be the CEO of some company or lead a nonprofit with a worthy cause. Or work at an animal rescue! I will excel at any of these, but I thought I was called to serve people in Congress! Why did you put me through all this just to lose by a sliver?" I was steaming and venting and not really listening. I got it out of my system and was ready to move forward. I came home, took a shower, stood in front of my bathroom mirror and stared at the yellow sticky notes HOPE and TRUST. I took them down. I was starting to look forward to whatever might come next in life to make a difference.

Soon, the daily vote count swung in our favor. And the next night, too. All of a sudden it looked like we were going to *win* by a sliver. Forty-three days after the election, and after a recount, I had won by a whopping 167 votes. I put the sticky notes back up again, thanked God for His favor, and apologized for not trusting Him! I know He understood, forgave, and knew I was going to struggle, but He loved me through it anyway.

As I look back, I realize that I felt God's protection throughout my young life, as He patiently waited for me to reach out to Him. I could not have survived this journey without the presence of a loving, faithful, wonderful God. Yes, the same God I was angry at for taking my dad. The same God I felt had abandoned me years later, when I was deeply hurt and betrayed. But when you feel stuck in an abyss, that is often when you receive God's gracious presence as never before.

I've always been drawn to the serenity prayer, used by Alcoholics Anonymous, which says, "God, grant me the serenity to accept the things I cannot change, the courage to change the things I can, and the wisdom to know the difference." I cannot change the past, I can only decide what I will do in the present moment to influence the future. Many things are beyond my control. I need to let them go and focus on what is within my grasp. So many times, I have needed the courage to pick myself up and push at a roadblock that seemed impossible but was, in fact, passable. Faith has given me the strength to push.

God has loved me, healed me, strengthened me, challenged me, and called me to greater purpose in life. He never left my side for a moment, in darkness, loss, and tragedy, as well as in triumph and success. What a gift! I am not here to press my faith on anyone, but I would not be honest if I left out this crucial part of my journey. God's light can dissolve the darkness and bring healing. He wants us to be whole and free. He wants us to live life with joy, love, and gratitude. He is so much more compassionate and loving than we could ever imagine, toward others as well as ourselves. I would not have endured and accomplished everything in my life without God. I would not have made it through the periods of darkness or through combat without Him.

I find kindred characters in so many Bible stories: Jacob, who physically wrestled all night with an angel before giving in and asking for God's blessing, which he received. Or Jonah, who ran away from God and ended up in the belly of a whale before he finally submitted. Or David, who wrote beautiful psalms filled with raw, honest expressions of his full emotions, which God answered by showing David renewed clarity of purpose, hope, and faith. As with any true relationship, I believe God wants us to be real, authentic, and honest with Him. It's not as if you can hide your emotions from Him—He is God, after all.

THESE DAYS, MY MOST FRUITFUL time with God is while I am out running. I often listen to worship music; I think, I pray, I swear (often in the same sentence—God knows my weakness of having a potty mouth and loves me anyway!); I de-stress, get new ideas, and come back refreshed and renewed. When I am in D.C., I try to schedule a run each week along the National Mall, starting at the U.S. Capitol, passing the Washington Monument and World War II Memorial, and reaching the Lincoln Memorial. When I get to the Lincoln Memorial, I say hi to Abe, read the Gettysburg Address, then take a moment to look back at the Capitol. I pray to be freed of the spirit of frustration with the dysfunction and replace it with the spirit of gratitude for the opportunity to serve. I pray for the president, the vice president, Congress, and all who serve. I pray for wisdom, unity, courage, and strength, along with the specifics of any problem we are facing. Then I run back to the Capitol and get to work, refreshed and renewed for the challenges and decisions that lie ahead.

The more I know God and His ways, the more I realize all I don't know, and I am okay with that. I pray you find your own faith in your own way, so you can know true peace and thrive, heal, love, forgive, and follow your own calling.

EIGHT

Do the Next Right Thing
(Part One)

"Can it be that you were put in this position for such a time as this?"

I WAS A TWENTY-EIGHT-YEAR-OLD CAPTAIN and a newly minted A-10 pilot when my squadron was ordered to Kuwait. Iraq's dictator, Saddam Hussein, was threatening to shatter the tenuous peace established after Desert Storm. Our mission was to fly A-10 combat patrols into southern Iraq to support the no-fly zone. I remember looking down at the big sand berm that separated Iraq's territory from Kuwait's during my first flight. As we crossed, my flight lead directed me to "fence in," the signal to prepare to enter enemy territory. I was a little nervous, but just like when I took off in the A-10 for the first time, I fenced in. (Yes, I did it afraid.) When I fenced out and crossed back into Kuwait, I was glad to have that rookie mission behind me. I didn't know it at the time, but according to the Pentagon, on that day, I became the first U.S. woman to fly a fighter jet in combat.

The Al Jaber base in Kuwait that housed my squadron had sustained substantial bomb damage during the brief war and wasn't set up to accommodate a female pilot. The men serving in combat support roles were housed in a tent city, while the women were sent to old dorms (which I thought was ridiculous, since we know how to do gender-integrated tent cities). All the pilots lived together in trailers in another part of the base called pilot town. But no one higher up had considered the possibility of a female pilot. The all-male squadron we were replacing had no desire to integrate me into pilot town, so when I arrived early as part of an advance team, I was dropped off at the dorms.

I immediately asked to move to pilot town. I didn't want to be isolated, and I had the same mission requirements as the male pilots. After much resistance, I was allowed to move into a trailer with a small bathroom and shower. Other trailers didn't have showers, so most pilots showered in a separate building.

We were trying to minimize water use, and I didn't want special treatment, so I said I would use the shower building like everyone else. The departing squadron hung a full, white sheet across the top of the last shower stall and wrote in large letters with duct tape: FEMALE. They told me to pull the sheet across whenever I entered the building. After my squadron arrived, we took down the sheet. It simply became a coed building with individual, private showers and toilets. Adults can figure out ways to accomplish the mission when they want.

In Kuwait, I was focused on working hard, flying well, blending in, and being one of the guys. The last thing I wanted was to complain about a "female" issue or policy. Outside of flying, I exercised (running and lifting weights), played cards, and helped with the music at the chapel.

Exercise was a key part of my day. It is important as an A-10 pilot to stay fit for many reasons. Most missions are physically demanding: a fellow A-10 pilot once described the intensity of military aviation as like "doing long division in the middle of a wrestling match." We also needed to be fit if we were shot down and had to evade capture and survive. Even if it wasn't essential for my profession, I would have exercised because I have been an athlete my whole life, and it was part of my physical, emotional, and spiritual well-being.

Before we deployed, the women were told that we could not show our legs and had to wear long pants at all times while on or off base. We were slated to be in Kuwait from mid-January to mid-April, when temperatures rise into the nineties or above. I was irritated to have to wear long pants, but I packed some workout tights to comply with the rule.

After my first time at the gym, I was informed that it was "inappropriate" for me to wear tights because they showed the "form of my legs." At first, I thought this was a prank. The male pilots were wearing shorts and T-shirts, tank tops, or no shirts, and the fact that I had to wear tights instead of shorts already grated on me. Now I was told I had to acquire baggy sweatpants. When I asked my boss to explain the rationale, his answer was "host nation sensitivities." We didn't want to offend our Kuwaiti hosts by having our servicewomen's legs or leg form visible.

We were a remote base, so there was no place to buy extra clothing. Somehow, I got my hands on a pair of large, gray Army sweatpants, big enough to fit three of me inside. If they wanted baggy, I was certainly complying. I used the drawstring to ensure they didn't fall down. The legs had thick bunches of material from the knees to my ankles. With all the folds and wrinkles, my fellow pilots said I looked like a shar-pei dog.

When I ran the roughly eight-mile loop around the base's runway, I had to wear my sweatpants. I was roasting and dehydrated, while my buddies cruised along in their comfortable shorts. Once the full squadron arrived, we played volleyball near our trailer compound, with no Kuwaiti in sight, but I still had to stay in my long, baggy sweats. Some of the guys had plumbing and electrical parts shipped over and turned a large vat into a hot tub, but I could not sit in it unless I wanted to wear my sweats. The most ridiculous example was when a Kuwaiti friend, an F-18 pilot who had been my classmate in pilot training back in the U.S., offered to take a group of us water-skiing in the Persian Gulf on our day off. I had to water-ski in my shar-pei sweats, which weighed about as much as I did after they got wet.

My anger about the "sweatpants policy" rose every day. Kuwait was a fairly moderate Muslim country. Unlike Saudi Arabia, it didn't impose complex restrictions on women's attire. I used to fight with my Kuwaiti F-18 pilot friend about these demeaning rules for U.S. servicewomen, until he told me that the Kuwaitis did not require it. It was an American military policy. (A senior general abruptly ended the sweatpants policy one year later in 1996 after I raised it again on my next deployment. I actually discussed it while chatting with his wife. He discovered it had no basis in any official rule or regulation. It was a classic example of military folklore.)

One day on base, I saw a publication for U.S. military personnel in the region. In addition to the A-10s in Kuwait, there were lots of U.S. military personnel scattered around. I looked at the front cover and saw a woman dressed in the traditional, black abaya with a black head scarf wrapped around her head. I did a double take, wondering why a Middle Eastern woman would be on the cover of an American military publication. As I looked closer, I realized it was an American woman. And not just any American, but an American military woman. The caption explained that this was the proper way to wear the abaya and head scarf when traveling off base in Saudi Arabia.

I was shocked. Something inside me was immediately convinced that this was wrong. And even though the rule didn't apply to me, it needed to be changed.

MY FATHER OCCASIONALLY TOOK ME to his law office on the weekends. I undoubtedly absorbed some lessons from him (maybe there is even an "advocacy" DNA strand) on how to build a case and win. He showed me you need to do your homework if you are going to persuade others and win an argument, in the courtroom or in life. Thus, however tempting it was to act, speak, or make a decision based on how I felt, versus examining the objective reality of a situation or listening to sage advice, I knew that if I didn't dig deep for the facts, only failure would follow. Without research, my feelings would remain just that, feelings, not a persuasive argument.

So, I was determined to find where this abaya policy came from and why. The first step was to figure out where the policy was written down, if at all, and who had the legal authority behind it? Who had signed off on it?

After calling around, I found an office that appeared to know about the abaya policy. They explained that service-women were required to wear it due to "the possibility of offending host nation [Saudi] sensitivities." I was told it was part of a Status of Forces Agreement between the U.S. and Saudi Arabia to allow U.S. military forces to be stationed in the kingdom. I asked to have the policy faxed to me so I could see it in writing.

I was amazed to discover that the same regulation that directed servicewomen to wear traditional Muslim garb also forbade men from wearing any local customary clothing. Huh? I called back the office to ask about the inconsistency, and they defended the policy as part of the requirement by the Saudis. "When in Saudi, do as the Saudis do." But if we were trying to blend in and look like locals, then both men and women should wear the customary garb. Discovering that our female troops in Saudi were indeed forced to wear an abaya and head scarf made the sweatpants policy in Kuwait seem like a minor inconvenience. At least I was only forced to wear Western-looking baggy sweatpants and not the garments of a faith I do not follow, while also representing the United States military.

It would be wrong and unconstitutional if every service member were required to wear a Christian cross or a Star of David or a Buddhist saffron robe, regardless of their faith, and U.S. taxpayers had to pay for it. But the policy was also a de facto endorsement of a backward Saudi culture where women are essentially considered the property of their male owner, first their fathers and then their husbands. At the time, and indeed until 2018, Saudi women could not drive. Until 2019, they could not travel without the written permission of a male relative. Any testimony they give in court is worth less than that of a man. Grown women can be punished for interacting with adult males who are not their relatives. And women must be fully covered. They have no choice. Welcome to the seventh century.

It is one thing to tolerate these medieval practices in the name of larger, strategic interests with Saudi Arabia. But not to impose these "cultural" practices on a member of the U.S. military who is there, risking her life, to protect and defend Saudi and U.S. interests in the region. What example were we setting for the Saudis regarding *our* country's values?

But while I believed that this policy was deeply wrong, I was in no position to change it. I continued to fly my missions and run in my baggy sweats, and wondered how I could do something. Until an unexpected opportunity arrived.

Secretary of Defense William Perry was scheduled to

visit the base and he wanted to meet with me, since I was the first woman flying combat sorties. I had a dilemma. If the SecDef asked me what it was like as a woman deploying to Kuwait to fly combat missions, should I tell him it is just fine, or do I raise the sweatpants policy or the abaya policy?

As his visit approached, I wrestled with what to do. I called a mentor of mine at Laughlin Air Force Base in Del Rio, Texas. Communications were very challenging at our little base. We did not have email. We only had a military tactical field phone, which we used to reach a military operator, who connected us with our friends and loved ones. The quality of the calls was poor, and the signals often dropped. There was a significant delay in the transmission, so you constantly stepped on each other's words. We would often resort to saying "over" when we were done so the other person knew they could talk next. I asked my mentor for his advice. He told me to read the Book of Esther in the Old Testament. I was not very familiar with the story, and I was a little annoyed he was turning our limited call into a Sunday school class. I thanked him and hung up, disappointed that it seemed I had to make this important decision alone.

With a bad attitude, I started the Book of Esther that night. What I discovered was a story that would change my life. (If you are a biblical scholar, please excuse my paraphrasing.) Esther was a young Israeli orphan living in the Persian Empire and being raised by her cousin Mordecai in the fifth century B.C. At the time, the Persian king, Xerxes (Ahasuerus), grew angry with his wife and decided to look for a new queen. The king's staff held a yearlong "beauty contest," where young virgin girls competed for the king's favor. At Mordecai's urging, Esther applied.

Esther was chosen to become the new queen, but Xerxes did not know she was Jewish. Haman the Agagite, a prominent prince, had a generations-long grudge against the Jews and convinced the king to sign an edict to wipe them out of Persia. Mordecai appealed to Esther to save her people, but Esther's intervention came with great risk. If anyone approached the king uninvited, even the queen, they could be put to death. The only way to be spared was if the king extended his scepter.

As Esther wrestled with what to do, Mordecai offered a profound insight: "Can it be that you were put in this position for such a time as this?" Could it be that Esther became the queen not to enjoy her life, but to risk her life to save her people from extinction? Esther decided to approach the king. The scepter was extended, Haman was hanged, and the Jews were saved.

When I read the line "Can it be that you were put in this position for such a time as this?" the words struck me. I am no Esther, but I had worked hard to become a pilot. Yet could it be that the very reason I was given the opportunity to become a fighter pilot was to be in a position to stand up against this denigrating and demeaning policy? I knew the answer, but I resisted it. When I sense I am called to do something that carries a high personal cost and has little chance of success, like most human beings, I struggle and look for any other possible avenue before finally giving in. I knew if I raised this issue with the secretary of defense, I would anger many people in the chain of command above me. I would be labeled a troublemaker by the military "tribe."

But Esther's story wouldn't leave me alone. After much prayer and consideration, I decided to follow her example and view this opportunity as an obligation to stand up for young female officers and enlisted troops who didn't have the platform I had. I talked to my squadron commander, and he completely supported me. I sensed he also believed the policies were wrong and wanted to give me an opportunity to bring it up with the secretary.

On the day of the official visit, my commander ensured I wasn't flying. But Secretary Perry ran late, our meeting was cut from his schedule, and he went directly to speak to the troops. My commander still wanted me to have my chance. He told the pilots on combat search and rescue alert to drive me to the speech site. I could ask my question during the public Q and A. My heart was racing. A public forum was very different from a private meeting. When it appeared that he was wrapping up, I raised my hand.

"Secretary Perry, I understand you just came from Saudi Arabia, meeting with Saudi leaders. Has there been any consideration to treating our female troops serving there with a little bit more dignity?" He knew exactly what I was talking about. He tried to sound sympathetic. "I will be honest with you," Perry began. "We haven't made a lot of progress in that area, but we won't give up." Pretty disappointing, a typical, political nonanswer.

A small group of reporters rushed over. What was I talking about? For a second I thought about explaining the stupid sweatpants policy, but I simply told them, "Well, there are a number of discriminatory and demeaning policies enforced on just our women over here in the name of host nation sensitivities, but the most egregious one is that servicewomen are forced to wear the full Muslim garb in Saudi Arabia." They asked why I was raising it, since I was stationed in Kuwait. I explained it was wrong, and it was my duty as an officer to fix things that are wrong. The SecDef finished, and they left.

That day, the Associated Press published a story entitled: "Perry Expects Extended U.S. Presence in Gulf." Halfway through, it mentioned my question to Perry and quoted his answer. Next thing I knew, my squadron commander was getting chewed out by everyone in the chain of command between him and the defense secretary. Someone wanted heads to roll for allowing me to ask this question and speak to the media about it. There was talk of firing the public affairs officer for not giving me proper media training and direction. Of course, two years earlier, when the Pentagon announced it was allowing women to train for combat flying, the top brass was happy to parade me in front of the press. In fact, the female pilots chosen to represent the policy change had received the same intensive media training as the top generals. As a result, I had more media experience and training than anyone on the base or four levels up my chain of command.

My question was not spontaneous, but well thought out and memorized, after a deliberate decision. The problem for the Air Force higher-ups was that I had done my homework, studied the laws and regulations, and they had no grounds to punish me. But I had violated the informal "tribal customs," and I needed to "pay" for my betrayal.

My operations officer was furious at me while most guys in the squadron thought it was cool that I had the "balls" to raise an issue with the SecDef, even if they couldn't relate.

I now know this is an often-typical military reaction to public controversy. Circle the wagons, blame and attack the one who spoke out, and pay zero attention to the actual issue raised. There is something deeply ingrained in military culture that defends "the way things are" to a fault. They believe if they change a policy after public embarrassment, everything will fall apart.

The military often says it desires transformational and innovative leaders, change agents, and leaders who ask questions. The reality is they eventually largely stop promoting this type of officer. Years later, when I was a student at the Air War College, I discovered that my Myers-Briggs personality type of ENTP (extrovert-intuitive-thinker-perceiver) was statistically nonexistent in the military above the rank of lieutenant colonel. That explained a lot!

My squadron commander stood by me, and the whole

thing eventually blew over. But of course, the policy didn't change.

After my squadron returned home, I continued to research the policy in my spare time and advocate to change it—this coincided with the same period when I played Crud, gave up dipping, was promoted to major, and endured the Ka-Ching antics of the A-10 Weapons School.

After several years, despite what I had been told, I discovered that the abaya policy was not codified in any documents between the U.S. and the Saudis. The Saudis had not officially requested that our female troops be covered or ride in the backs of vehicles. Nor had our State Department made any such request. In fact, officials at the State Department said it was an internal U.S. military policy.

I was appalled and elated. Appalled, because for nearly five years I thought this entire policy had been agreed to by diplomats at the State Department to appease the Saudis and allow the U.S. access to Saudi military bases. And elated, because now I knew where to focus my attention to get these mandates changed.

The military is a boundless bureaucracy with regulations, policies, directives, instructions, and manuals for everything we do. The upside of this system is that almost everything is written down. After exhaustive research, I discovered that the only place this was written down was in the local dress and personal appearance regulation signed by a two-star general on the ground in Saudi Arabia. The regulation that was faxed to me in 1995!

For years, commanders in this slot rotated in and out on short-term deployments, passing down regulations and policies to their equally short-term replacements. Sometimes, a new commander inherited a batch of policies and added his own bureaucratic tweaks—or his staff did. If you have experience in the military, it's not hard to picture how one irrational rule can morph into a set of inflexible mandates. Over the years, the policy went from wearing conservative civilian clothes if you were off base, to wearing the abaya but not the head scarf, to wearing both the abaya and the head scarf, and then to sitting in the back seat of the car and having a male escort.

I often speculated on how the full complement of rules came about following a slippery slope of what I call bureaucratic policy creep. Years later, I found out thanks to one of my superior officers. Then–Colonel Lawrence Stutzriem discovered that the abaya mandate originated with a sergeant in the motor pool! After an exhaustive search, he could find no evidence that it was ever "vetted at any higher level." Yet despite that, the policy became the status quo, and the highest echelons of the military fiercely defended it.

Still, even the military's own reasoning for the abaya policy kept shifting. When I started asking questions, the answer I got was "cultural sensitivities to our hosts." But after a Navy destroyer, the USS *Cole*, was bombed in the fall of 2000, the policies were also categorized as "force protection." That meant that if you opposed the abaya policy, you could be accused of "risking the lives of U.S. troops."

But the force-protection argument was fundamentally flawed. Put the three policies together, and the logic was doomed: (1) Women had to wear full Muslim garb. (2) Men were forbidden to wear customary Muslim garb. (3) Women needed a male escort at all times. Even if I actually succeeded in blending in and looking like a Saudi woman, I was being accompanied by an escort whose haircut and demeanor clearly identified him as an American military man. Therefore, I look like a Saudi woman "hanging out" with an American GI, and Saudi women have been stoned to death for less (death by stoning is a sanctioned punishment for adultery in Saudi Arabia).

Did the military also really think that a terrorist waiting with an IED (improvised explosive device) or rocket launcher by the side of the road would suddenly refuse to detonate his weapon because he noticed a woman wearing a head scarf riding in the back of an American SUV? The final argument I often heard was that the religious police could harass, attack, hit, throw acid at, or jail a woman if she did not wear an abaya and head scarf. In other words, it was dangerous out there, and we couldn't put our poor, vulnerable female troops at risk, so we must cover them, not unlike Afghan women under the Taliban. But wait a minute: Isn't Saudi Arabia one of our allies? And didn't we protect them when Saddam Hussein invaded Kuwait in 1990? And aren't we stationed in Saudi in part to help them? My position was that if was that dangerous for me to leave the base, then I didn't need an abaya to protect myself, I needed my weapon. And if we couldn't ensure the protection and equal treatment of *all* our troops off base, then the men shouldn't leave base, either, or we needed to find another country for our troops.

When people tried to justify the cultural-respect angle, I told them I agreed with respecting cultures when it came to things like taking your shoes off when entering a home, not shaking with your left hand, and so on. In other words, when the cultural issue doesn't violate the basic tenets that we observe as a nation and that we in the military wear the uniform to protect. But in this case, the cultural norms treated women like property. It is not a perfect analogy, but consider a scenario in which the U.S. deployed its troops to South Africa during the height of apartheid. Would we have directed our African American troops to endure the same barbaric restrictions as black South Africans because of the need to respect "cultural sensitivities"? Such "rules" would, rightly, be seen as galling and intolerable, and contrary to everything that we stand for and our military fights for. It's hard to see the difference between that and the demeaning rules that were forced on our servicewomen in Saudi Arabia, which practices its own version of female apartheid.

My next phase in this battle was a complete surprise. About the time I discovered the origin of the abaya directive—that it was only written in the two-star general's local policy—I was notified that I would be sent to Saudi Arabia. Now, I was going to be subjected to the abaya policy myself.

NINE

Do the Next Right Thing
(Part Two)

"I have a problem with policies that treat servicewomen like property instead of military members."

I WAS BEING ORDERED TO Saudi Arabia for a year to direct combat search and rescue operations for our pilots flying inside southern Iraq. The last place on earth I wanted to be was Saudi Arabia, although I knew the mission mattered more than my own views. My one shot at not deploying was if the two-star general in charge decided that I was not the right person for his team. He had asked me to do a phone interview.

I was advised by my commander at the time not to bring up the abaya policy during the interview. You can discuss it at a later date, I was told. The general and I had a professional exchange about the mission, but my tone was flat. I requested a second call where I shared my real issue.

I told him that I had been fighting for five years to change the abaya policy, adding, "I have a problem with policies that treat servicewomen like property instead of military members. It is wrong on so many levels, demeaning to the troops, bad for good order and discipline, and an abandonment of American values."

The general replied that there was nothing he could do about it since it was above his pay grade. I advised him that it was in fact his policy, handed down to him by his predecessors. He couldn't believe it, but I told him I had done all the research and it was true.

I also said that if I were forced to go off base to do my job, as a Christian, an officer, and a fighter pilot, I was not going to put on an abaya. The general responded, "Fair enough," adding that he respected my conviction and wanted someone with spunk and character on his team. He asked me to send him my research and promised to review it and see what he could do.

I was hired.

I began to feel positive about this new assignment. After fighting this policy from the outside, I was going to be on the staff of the person who could actually change the rules once and for all.

By early November, my belongings and furniture were packed up and put into storage, and my dog had been "deployed" to my brother's house. I had two military-issue green duffel bags ready to go. Then I got an email from my Air Force chaplain, who had already deployed to Saudi. He wrote that I would be directed to wear an abaya as soon as I arrived. On the two-hour drive to my new base in a convoy of U.S. vehicles in the middle of the night, I would be ordered to sit in the back seat and wear an abaya and head scarf.

I was stunned but not concerned, because the general had said he respected my conviction to not don an abaya. I sent his chief of staff an email to remind him of our conversation. I would wear a dark, loose-fitting, long-sleeve shirt and pants and would sit in the back of the car, but I wasn't planning to wear the abaya, or anything like it.

I sent the email on Sunday, November 12, 2000, at 10:43 P.M. I was scheduled to depart Tuesday night. The subject line was, "Potential Problem Upon Arrival in Theater." In the last paragraph, I wrote: "Sir, I have no intention of making a scene, but I thought it was important to reiterate my conviction so that no one is surprised. I am a Christian American soldier, not a Muslim Saudi woman. I look forward to contributing to the OSW mission." It was signed: "V/R Maj Martha McSally"—V/R meaning "very respectfully."

A little over six hours later, I received the colonel's reply, which CC'ed the two-star general. "Major McSally," he began, "I read your email with some concern." After noting that, "I'm sure your election to forego the opportunities of learning about middle eastern culture firsthand did not come easily," he added, "You are not free, however, to determine that the policy does not apply to you on your way to Eskan [the base where I was assigned]. It would be regrettable if you were to choose to place yourself personally at risk by ignoring force protection measures. It would also be extremely regrettable if you were to place yourself at risk professionally by choosing to violate specific command directives. I encourage you to carefully consider your actions." He ended the email by writing, "Like many things we deal with in our environment, the middle eastern culture presents all of us with challenges."

It was now Monday morning. It was clear what he meant by "extremely regrettable" if I put myself "at risk professionally" by violating "command directives." I had witnessed troops dealing with the consequences of disobeying an order. The Uniform Code of Military Justice (UCMJ) was swift and severe. If I chose to follow my conscience, I would be taken up on charges and my career in the Air Force would be over. I had about thirty-six hours to decide.

My gut reaction was to disobey and suffer the consequences, following my oath of office and what I believed was right.

I called the office of my boss in Washington, then–Major General Michael Moseley, and asked to meet with him. In person, the general told me he was going to share some advice. I told him I wasn't asking for advice but just warning him he would get a call when I landed and was taken up on charges for refusing to don Muslim garb. He said I was going to get it anyway.

He asked me to consider my two options and which one had the best potential to change the policy. In one scenario, I would be arrested, court-martialed, and kicked out of the Air Force. He predicted that in this scenario, the policy would never change. My other option was to comply with the abaya policy "one time," build trust with the commander, and offer a solution to reverse the policy, which General Moseley also found offensive. Change was within my grasp, all I had to do was submit to the policy "one time." He was from Texas and talked with a drawl, summarizing his point: "If you want to light yourself on fire to make your point, that's your choice. Think about it tonight and make a good, thoughtful decision and let me know what you decide."

I would end my career, but not change the policy. This potential haunted me. I called a close friend to talk it through and spent a lot of time praying. By morning, I had decided to go against my gut and take my general's advice. Less than twelve hours before my plane was scheduled to depart, I received a new email from another colonel, a JAG (Judge Advocate General) lawyer in Saudi Arabia. She admonished me that "the requirement to wear the abaya . . . constitutes a valid, lawful order which you violate at your own peril." It was hard to be more direct or threatening than that. I sent a reply communicating my decision, but making it clear I had decided to comply not because I was afraid of the professional threats and consequences they had conveyed, but "because I am committed to influencing a change in this policy." Boy, it had the potential to be a long year.

My plane landed in the middle of the night. The women were handed black abayas and head scarves and told to sit in the back seat of the car. I took a deep breath and put on my abaya. I was the highest-ranking person in my Suburban and the only woman. I sat in the back seat.

DURING MY FIRST WEEK, I saw a paper taped to the wall outside the colonel's office with a picture of a servicewoman wearing the abaya and head scarf. I read what was written below. It stated, "the religious police, or 'General Presidency of the Promotion of Virtue and Prevention of Vices' is concerned about attire and conduct during off-base recreational trips to Riyadh." The next sentence noted, "Their patrols have observed incidents in which personnel have engaged in behavior which is offensive to host nation religious sensitivities." Chief among what was categorized as "offensive behavior" were women not wearing a headcover, not buttoning their abayas to the top, and wearing red lipstick, and "women and men eating and walking together." The paper then stated how women were to dress, adding "the Koran dictates females [sic] hair will be completely covered," what makeup they should wear, and then had a separate bullet point stating, "Men and women should not walk or eat together unless married. If a group has only one female, she should walk with a single male, who should be identified as her husband if questioned." The summary noted that U.S. military personnel, as "guests" of the Saudi government, were "allowed certain concessions in regards to religious requirements set forth in the Koran." It ended with "See page two for example of properly worn headscarf."

This one-page document was staggering. It instructed U.S. female military personnel to comply with policies so as not to offend the religious police. But these "Mutawa," as the Saudis called them, bore no resemblance to Western concepts of law enforcement. They carried sticks to beat women who they deemed insufficiently covered, assaulted children, chased vehicles when they believed their occupants had violated religious codes, and were known for dragging women by their head scarves to place them under arrest. These were the men we were being directed not to offend. This was the system that U.S. female military personnel were being told to adhere to. More than that, our military policy had now been enlarged to state that if a man and a woman chose to eat or walk together in public and were stopped and questioned, both were directed to claim that they were husband and wife. This was presented as necessary in order to comply with the Saudi interpretation of Islamic sharia law, which forbade men and women who were not close relatives from appearing together in public.

One of the Air Force's three core values is "Integrity First." Yet here I was looking at a policy directing us both to lie and to follow religious "dictates" from the Koran, when our country was founded on separation of church and state. I was amazed that no one around me seemed to think there was anything wrong with this directive. Perhaps it was because the command leadership was overwhelmingly filled with men, and nobody was trying to throw black cloaks over them.

Now that I was actually in Saudi, I believed there were easy changes that could be made to the policy that would make it more reasonable and appropriate. Servicewomen should not have to wear the abaya when traveling on duty off base, such as when I arrived in the country or traveled through a commercial airport. Simply have a dress code of long pants or long skirt and a long-sleeve, loose-fitting shirt. For travel to a Saudi military facility for official business (assuming the Saudis would "allow" a woman to inter-act with them), a woman should not have to put an abaya and head scarf on over her U.S. military uniform and then remove it. Let women travel in their uniforms, just like their male counterparts.

If the general made these alterations, it would greatly im-prove conditions for the female troops.

I made an appointment to see the general and typed up a proposed new policy. When I entered the general's office, also there, waiting for me, were both his chief of staff and his JAG colonel. That should have been my first sign that this was not going to be the meeting I had hoped for, but I pressed on. It very quickly became a one-way conversa-tion about how wrong I was to care about this policy. I was attacked personally, three on one, for being so passionate. They demanded to know "what is the matter with you?" Why are you so "obsessed" with this policy? They insisted that "all the other women" were "fine" with it. Why can't you just be a good airman and follow orders for the mission "like everyone else"? Repeatedly, I was told that I was the only one who "cares" about this.

It was one of my worst moments in the military. I gave up and was eventually dismissed.

IN THE NEW YEAR, THE general ordered me to fly to the U.S. to attend a search and rescue conference, which meant wearing the abaya. My deputy drove me to the airport, and

I checked in. Then, like many Saudi women, immediately after boarding the plane, I peeled off my cloak and head scarf. While I was in D.C., I showed some of my friends my taxpayer-funded, government-issued, military-enforced Muslim garb.

When I was back in Saudi, Ed Pound, a reporter with *USA Today* (who heard about the abaya from a congressional staffer), emailed me, asking if I would speak to him about the abaya issue. I agonized about what to do. I had complied with the policy for almost six months and could have easily complied for another six and let it go. I certainly had nothing to gain from going public with a complaint. But I decided that this was an opportunity to tell people about it, and maybe someone else would join me as a wingman in the fight, since, as pilots say, I was out of airspeed and altitude and needed help.

I informed my supervisor about the email from the reporter, and during a spring trip to the U.S., I decided to talk to him. I sent an email to my boss informing him of my decision while I was in the U.S., and I also contacted the Air Force Public Affairs office at the Pentagon to tell them I was going to do this interview, and it would be controversial. I invited them to sit in, but they declined. Ed was really engaged and interested and asked for photos. I was at a search and rescue conference in Las Vegas when my phone rang. It was my mom. The story was on the front page of *USA Today,* above the fold. And it was big. The headline was: "Saudi Rules Anger Top Air Force Pilot." The next call was from my supervisor in Saudi Arabia. He told me to get on the next airplane back. His voice was terse and short. Strap in, McSally, I told myself.

As I walked through the airport, I saw my photo at every newsstand. On the long flight overseas, a guy sitting next to me was reading *USA Today* and said he thought "that fighter pilot" was courageous but somewhat crazy taking on the military like this. I eventually confessed that the "crazy pilot lady" was his seatmate.

I passed through immigration and met my supervisor on the other side. He had a plastic bag in his hand with an abaya and head scarf in it. He pushed it into my torso and barked out: "Put it on, now!" I was a major and was about to become a lieutenant colonel. He was a lieutenant colonel. And somehow these policies, and my questioning of them, had this American man barking at me to put on a full, black Muslim outfit as he stood there in his khakis and polo shirt. That's how distorted these policies made things.

I wasn't about to disobey the order now. So, for the fifth time, I wore the abaya and hijab and sat in the back seat of the car, trying to make small talk. All I got was: "You will report to the J3's office [the colonel in my chain of command] at 0730 in uniform for your first counseling session."

In the morning, I reported to the colonel's office. He dressed me down for my unprofessional behavior, particularly for how I chose to speak to *USA Today*. He saw me as a poor leader, a bad example to the troops, disloyal to the chain of command, you name it. I repeated my case to him, but he didn't want to hear it. After he finished "counseling" me, I was dismissed.

The next tactic tried against me was to suggest that I needed a mental health evaluation and that something must be wrong with me because I chafed so strongly at wearing an abaya and a hijab.

But I heard from female diplomats in the U.S. embassy, who thought I was 100 percent right. They said they hung the article in their office and cheered for me to prevail. This countered the folklore that the military's policy was for "diplomatic" reasons. I learned that the embassy definitely was not encouraging this policy, and American female diplomats did not wear abayas while on official duty representing the U.S. government. Off duty, some women assigned to the embassy chose to wear the abaya and some chose not to—there was no policy mandating its wear. They were not allowed to drive, but they also were not directed to sit in the back seat of the car. They had no idea why the military had created these directives. These women explained that when an American woman donned the abaya and head scarf, they felt she was essentially submitting herself to Saudi religious customs as if she were a Muslim, inviting harassment from the zealots. It was wonderful to have diplomats—women and men—behind me.

Within a few days of the *USA Today* article, a bipartisan group of five U.S. senators (including Susan Collins, with whom I served in the Senate) asked the secretary of defense for a full policy review. Some military officers emailed me or quietly pulled me aside to say they supported me. A few were colonels. But I wanted to say, don't tell *me* what you think, tell the general. Meanwhile, I hoped the policy review would go my way.

IN THE U.S., JOHN WHITEHEAD, who led the nonprofit Rutherford Institute, which provides legal support for people fighting for our constitutional freedoms, saw the *USA Today* piece and reached out to offer me legal support. At first, I was confused—I thought he meant as a defense lawyer in case the military charged me with something. He explained that he believed the abaya policy was unconstitutional, and the Rutherford Institute would provide free legal representation if I wanted to file a lawsuit against the military.

I had never heard of someone in uniform suing the military. (I later discovered it does happen, and several important policy changes, such as allowing women to serve on Navy ships and stopping the practice of kicking women out of the military when they became pregnant, came about after legal challenges.) I asked exactly whom I would be suing, and he explained that it needed to be the first civilian in the chain of command, because you can't sue a military member. My chain went from the two-star to a four-star to the secretary of defense. So, what we were talking about here was *Martha McSally v. Donald Rumsfeld*. I thanked John Whitehead for reaching out, but I was not interested in going nuclear just yet. *McSally v. Rumsfeld*. Now, that was funny.

Over the summer, I grew very discouraged. I was isolated and feeling worn down. A new colonel, Lawrence Stutzriem, arrived, and instead of buying all the nonsense about how I was wrong, needed to be sent for a mental health evaluation, and needed to be squashed, he listened with an open mind, respectfully heard me out, and started questioning the policy himself. He ultimately supported my efforts and stood up against the insanity, a very unpopular but deeply principled stance. He was the unexpected wingman I needed at just the right time.

By August, some friends in the Pentagon told me it looked like the Defense Department policy review would make the case for keeping the status quo. The story of Esther came back to me. I called John Whitehead. I informed the new commander that a lawsuit would be filed in two weeks, hoping they might change the policy first. We planned to present my lawsuit on September 12, 2001, but that didn't happen.

The 9/11 attacks, plus fifteen of the nineteen hijackers being Saudi citizens, put us in lockdown, while at the same time we were going full tilt to plan the initial air campaign in Afghanistan. After the war in Afghanistan started, celebrities and other national figures such as First Lady Laura Bush talked about how U.S. forces were freeing the Afghan people from the oppression of the Taliban. Women were no longer being forced to wear the burqa. I remember sitting in the Saudi-based operations center watching news reports and yelling: "Am I the only one who sees the irony in this?

The very people who are helping free Afghan women from wearing the burqa are actually forced to wear a burqa by our own military!" You couldn't make this stuff up.

I extended my deployment for a month, then decided to file the lawsuit a few days before I departed in December 2001. My old boss, General Moseley, who had advised me to wear the abaya one time, had been promoted and was now commanding the air war over Afghanistan. Moseley himself had never been comfortable with the policy and had advocated for changing it. Indeed, he had told me during our initial meeting before I deployed that the abaya mandate was out of bounds for a professional military. But at this point, most of the military establishment was digging in to defend it.

I wanted to tell him in person that I was going to sue and wished it hadn't come to this. He said he wished that I "didn't pick this timing," since we were at war.

I replied, "Sir, with all due respect, I didn't pick this timing. Military leadership did. If they had listened to the experts at the embassy, these policies would not even exist. They could have been changed when I addressed the issue with Secretary Perry in 1995. Or in 1996, '97, '98, or '99. Or when I sent the research to the general in the summer of 2000. Or when the USA Today article came out in April 2001. Or during the Pentagon policy review. Or even once they realized that practices like this were what we were freeing the women of Afghanistan from. I didn't pick this timing. The leaders who failed to do the right thing picked this timing, and I have shown ample patience. I have nothing to gain. I complied with the policy for thirteen months. But I believe this is wrong and I am not going to stop fighting until it is overturned. Thanks for hearing me out. Tell the Pentagon I will see them in court."

Thankfully, General Moseley didn't try to dissuade me. He understood the value of my quest. Now, I hoped to find a few more General Moseleys.

The lawsuit, *McSally v. Rumsfeld*, was filed, and I left for my next assignment. Media requests poured in. People were fascinated that a female A-10 pilot was suing Donald Rumsfeld over wearing Muslim garb. When I arrived in the U.S., it was a whirlwind of TV, radio, and print interviews. *Good Morning America*, the *Today* show, Fox News, CNN, the *Washington Post*, *People*.

Lesley Stahl from *60 Minutes* wanted to run a short piece. I told her the whole story. By the end, she made our interview the lead story. After *60 Minutes*, the Pentagon altered its policy—servicewomen were no longer required to wear the abaya but were instead "strongly encouraged" for their safety. This was ridiculous. The reality is that in the military, if your commander "strongly encourages" you to do something, especially for your safety, you will feel extraordinary pressure to comply.

The TV series *JAG* even aired an episode on the abaya issue, which was based on the truth but not totally accurate.

It featured a female Navy pilot who decked a local Saudi guy when he tried to demand she cover up after she made an emergency landing on Saudi soil. Perhaps they were channeling my feelings.

After my fight made national news, I was contacted by retired Army four-star general Barry McCaffrey. He had commanded the ground forces during Desert Storm, and he said he completely agreed with my efforts. He believed the present situation was due to a failure of military leadership. General McCaffrey explained that when the Saudis quietly tried to pressure him to put restrictions on our female troops during Desert Storm, he refused to make any concessions. He thought perhaps another general along the way had given in and decided to adopt these awful policies. He wrote an affidavit in support of my lawsuit. Meanwhile, in one Hog Log thread, posters wrote that I was a "POS" and should be sent to Afghanistan to be taken out by a dumb bomb or walk through "downtown Saudi" and make myself a target for any terrorist "looking to kill Americans." Fortunately, I didn't see those comments until nine months later. By then, much had changed.

IN JANUARY, CONGRESSMAN JIM LANGEVIN, who had grown up in my Rhode Island neighborhood and knew my family, invited me to attend President George W. Bush's State of the Union address to Congress. The Rutherford

Institute alerted the media. When the president referenced women's rights and equality around the world, the TV cameras cut to me and flashed my name and rank. Many people thought I had been invited by the president.

The court case was dragging on with motions to dismiss and other typical legal delays. I started thinking, we have three branches of the government: the first one (executive) failed, the second one (judicial) was taking a long time, so why not turn to the third one (legislative), which has oversight of the executive branch? Since I had been a legislative fellow on Capitol Hill the year before deploying to Saudi Arabia, I knew what it would take to get a legislative solution. I talked with some Capitol Hill friends and we thought, why not add an amendment to the yearly defense bill to overturn the abaya policies? My court complaint had already enumerated what needed to be changed: not being allowed to drive; sitting in the back seat of a vehicle; being ordered to have a male escort and to lie, claiming a husband-wife relationship; and donning the abaya. We decided to focus our legislative efforts on the abaya policy, believing if that was removed, the others would follow.

Incredibly, ten days after we had drafted the amendment, the House held a debate and a vote on it as a free-standing bill. Representatives Heather Wilson, Jim Langevin, and John Hostettler made that happen and will always have my thanks. I was in the House Gallery as Democrats and Republicans spoke about why we should abolish the policy for the sake of women's rights and religious freedom. Both sides agreed, and the bill passed unanimously. I recalled my first month in Saudi Arabia, when the general in charge, Gene Renuart, raised his voiced and mocked me, saying: "You are the only one who cares about this!"

I said to myself with a smile: "I am *not* the only one who cares about this. Today it is me and the 435 representatives of the people of the United States who care about this, you jerk."

Now it had to succeed in the Senate, and I was fortunate to have a champion in New Hampshire senator Bob Smith. We worked hard to make it happen, but when it came time to finalize the House and Senate bills into one document for the president to sign, I got word that the Pentagon was working to insert a vast loophole that would effectively kill the implementation of our legislation and codify the abaya mandate in law. I started a one-woman lobbying campaign aimed at the key members of the House and Senate Armed Services Committees, who would determine the final bill. And I wanted to make sure that the man leading the charge to torpedo the amendment, Representative John McHugh, knew that he would be viewed as the U.S. congressman who put U.S. servicewomen "back in the burqa." I called McHugh's office, and next thing I knew, McHugh was on the line. I walked him through the issues and asked him to please support the language in the bill, without any loophole. He promised to think about it. Ultimately, McHugh did not ask for a single change. No loopholes. Just like that, the battle was over.

In September 2002, I deployed again to Saudi Arabia with my team. On December 2, 2002, I stayed up late to watch C-SPAN and see President Bush sign the annual defense bill into law, which included my abaya prohibition provision. My unit left Saudi at the end of December, and I hoped to not return any time soon. But we were quickly recalled to prepare for the Iraq War. This time someone got a bright idea to not let me deploy into Saudi with my team because I was a troublemaker. I was diverted to Qatar and raised a stink to rejoin my team. Eventually, cooler heads and mission focus prevailed. Once again, I landed in the middle of the night and was met by a female staff sergeant. My processing paperwork was spread on the hood of a jeep, and we went through it with a flashlight. The last thing she did was to hand me a piece of paper and say this was a copy of a law stating that said I did not have to wear an abaya or head scarf when traveling off base.

Our legislation required each servicewoman to be given a copy of the law within forty-eight hours of arriving in Saudi Arabia. This staff sergeant had no idea how much this piece of paper meant to me, or my role. I felt a flood of emotion. I looked up at the stars and whispered to myself: "It's finally over. We won."

In October 2019, now as a U.S. senator, I returned to Saudi Arabia for the first time since I was on active duty. I wore long pants and a long-sleeve shirt, and I drove a car. It was a truly great day.

GETTING IN THE DRIVER'S SEAT of that car in Western clothes without an abaya, more than twenty-four years after I first began the abaya battle, was the fulfillment of one of my favorite personal maxims: don't walk by a problem. In 1995, I could have walked by that picture of the service-woman in an abaya and ignored my conviction that it was wrong. Or I could have rationalized that it wasn't my problem, since at that moment it didn't apply to me. If we are honest with ourselves, we all have times when we are guilty of walking by a problem. Each of us can probably recall an instance when we should have spoken up or taken action, but rationalized that it wasn't our problem, or we didn't have the time or ability to deal with it.

To make a difference in the world, we need people who are willing to follow their convictions and stand up for what is right. This often requires moral courage and often comes at personal cost. It's important to be prepared and to be willing to pay the price. But at the end of the day, each of us is the sum of our life choices.

Our responsibility is even greater if those affected by the issue cannot fight for themselves. It took almost a decade, but I was humbled by the thought that, not unlike Esther, perhaps I was put in a position for such a time as this.

TEN

Thrive Through the Darkness

"It is possible to live and thrive through the darkness, trusting that the darkness can't last forever and that the night will end."

AFTER MY DAD DIED, WE got a rambunctious, precious golden retriever puppy named Casey. In a beautiful way, he served as an antidote to my loss. Casey ran with me to help me train for high school cross-country and track. He was relentless. In the summer when I arrived home from work, Casey would bolt to my closet, "fetch" my running shoes, and badger me until I took him racing on the beach.

When he was young, Casey started having seizures. Medicine controlled them, but it was difficult to watch when his body jerked and his mouth frothed. The seizures stopped for a while, until my junior year in high school. In the middle of the night, I heard him thrashing on the kitchen floor. I sprinted from my bedroom to comfort him, but this time, the seizure didn't subside. I carried my best buddy wrapped in a blanket to the car and cried uncontrollably as my mom rushed us to the vet. I knew in my spirit that I was going to lose him. There was nothing the vet could do, except keep him sedated. I remember petting and kissing Casey as he lay unconscious in a crate. I was devastated. Casey had been my constant, joyful companion.

Casey's death propelled me back into a profound state of sorrow. Grief is not unusual for people who love their animals and are blessed with that deep bond, but these feelings encompassed more than the loss of Casey. I did not understand it at the time, but I had not fully grieved the loss of my dad, more than four years before.

During my high school years, I was driven to succeed and excel, but I also acted out, rebelled, and got into minor trouble, my way of making my grief visible. It was tiring to keep it all up. For example, I would stay out late with friends, make a pot of coffee to study for an exam in an advanced class, sleep a little, ace the exam, then run seven miles at cross-country practice.

I also made a deal with my mom: if I kept a 4.0 GPA, I could skip school when I wanted. So, I was absent a lot. I felt it was a waste of time to sit in class when I could read the textbook and take the test. A few amazing teachers saw beneath the tough exterior to the struggling kid inside and tried to help me find my way. But I had built a house of cards, and Casey's death caused it to collapse.

When you have not gone through all the healthy steps of grieving, other losses can produce a disproportionate experience. I wanted my dad to be with me and hold me as I wept over the loss of my faithful dog. If he couldn't be here on earth, then maybe I should go to be with him and Casey instead. I needed help processing all that I felt, but I did not know how to ask.

I now understand that these dynamics are quite normal for a kid whose world has been turned upside down by the death of a parent. But the pain felt overwhelming, and I just wanted it to stop. In an impulsive moment of despair, I downed some pills and ended up in the hospital, drinking charcoal and having my stomach pumped. It was a cry for help. I had counseling and interventions, but what had the greatest impact was a quote from Eugene O'Neill's play, *The Great God Brown*, shared with me by a compassionate counselor: "Why am I afraid to dance, I who love music and rhythm and grace and song and laughter? Why am I afraid to live, I who love life and the beauty of flesh and the living colors of the earth and sky and sea? Why am I afraid to love, I who love love? Why am I afraid, I who am not afraid?" The message I heard was that no one could fix this, there was not some magic repair. Instead, I, who loved life, had to find my own way to push forward and work through my emotions and grief along the way.

I poured my energy into achieving to make my dad proud. I finished that difficult year with a 4.0 GPA and learned to throw the javelin. (Ironically, after all my years of swimming and running, in the fall, I was recruited by colleges for throwing a spear.) But while I was achieving on the outside, I remained a grieving girl on the inside.

My best emotional salve was running. It also helped that my first high school cross-country and track coach was very much of a father figure to me. But during my difficult junior year, he moved on to a coaching position at a college. It was hard to see him go, but his replacement seemed nice enough . . . and I transferred my trust to this new coach.

In the beginning, I valued his attention and encouragement, particularly coming immediately after such a traumatic time. It was no secret I was an extremely vulnerable, fatherless girl, and my coach took advantage of that and crossed the line. Instead of just verbal encouragement, he started to show physical affection. I was pretty naïve and innocent, so this was very confusing coming from a thirty-eight-year-old man in a position of authority, who was supposed to be guiding and mentoring me. He assured me it was okay, and said that we had a special relationship, which included showing physical affection for each other. He gradually pushed me for more. I was deeply uncomfortable, but I trusted him and eventually stopped resisting.

Predators often "sniff out" the "right" person to prey upon and create circumstances that can be really destabilizing for the victim. At first, I thought this man truly cared for me. But once I succumbed to his sexual abuse, my thoughts narrowed to one thing: survival. I taught myself to "check out" mentally and disassociate from what was going on. By the time I recognized what was really happening, it was too late. I felt ashamed and foolish, and he found ways to mock me for it.

For Christmas that year, he bought me a box of chocolate-covered cherries and laughed uproariously when I opened them. To this day, I cannot bear to look at a box of chocolate-covered cherries. When I tried to stop the abuse, he threatened to "go after" my best friend. I learned later that I wasn't the first fatherless high school girl he had manipulated and abused, and I am pretty sure I wasn't the last. Toward the end of my senior year, I found the strength to begin to untangle myself from him. He responded by informing me that the law for statutory rape in Rhode Island only applied if I was sixteen or younger, so, as a seventeen-year-old, I had no options. If I decided to tell anyone what was going on, he wouldn't have broken any laws. That is the hallmark of a predator, keeping their prey quiet and living in fear and shame. I finally found the courage to tell a school counselor what was happening. She was deeply distressed, ignored my request to say nothing, and instead went to the school leaders, who immediately fired him. She was willing to stand up for me and do the right thing at a time when many people in society chose to say nothing when alerted to similar abuses.

But this was also 1984. It was an era when abusers simply moved on to other jobs and what had happened was hushed up. Today, every few months, another school sends out a deeply regretful letter to alumni acknowledging past inappropriate sexual behavior by a faculty or staff member. My school did just that in May 2019, following a thorough investigation, after I publicly shared what had happened to me.

However, the fact that he was gone didn't mean I had been freed from the damage he did to me.

A HUGE DRAW OF THE Air Force Academy was its location nearly two thousand miles away from Rhode Island in Colorado. Although I had been accepted to other universities closer to home, the academy seemed like a great way to have a fresh start. I thought the challenge, discipline, and

opportunities would be good for me, and as an added benefit, I would be far from the man who had abused me. I now
realize you can change geography and physically remove
yourself from an abuser, but your wounds still get on the
plane with you.

When I returned to Rhode Island on school breaks and
later on military leave, I was always afraid that I would run
into my former coach. Sometimes I would see an adult man
with similar features and do a double take, my heart racing,
only to sigh in relief when I realized it wasn't him.

I ENVISIONED MILITARY LIFE AS a safe place for me to
channel my energy, be a part of something important, serve
the greater good, and meet my potential. And it was all that
and more for me for twenty-six years. But at the same time,
the Air Force was not always a safe haven.

During my early years in uniform, I was harassed,
abused, assaulted, and raped, like countless other women
and some men who have served their country. Yes, raped.

My story is not unique. While it benefits no one to delve
into the lurid details of each of my personal experiences, I
do think it is important to shine a light on the overall dynamics of these dark episodes so that other people—and
institutions—can learn from them and can work to end
abuse and assault, as well as to compassionately assist
victims.

In many ways, the hostile environment I faced as a young

Air Force pilot began at the academy, which first admitted women in 1976. I can't put my finger on how it happened, but it seemed as if many male cadets, who previously had no issues with strong mothers or sisters, or having a female class president or valedictorian, finished basic training with a deep resentment toward their female classmates. It didn't help that women constituted a small minority, about 10 percent of the academy when I was a cadet. Male cadets routinely placed their female peers in three categories: bitches, dykes, or sluts. (It also didn't help that former Air Force Chief of Staff and General Curtis LeMay was quoted in 1986 as having said, "Married Air Force women lack commitment and single ones are 'queer.'") If a woman was focused on succeeding, competing, and beating the male cadets, she was a bitch. If a woman had a relationship with a male cadet, she was categorized as a slut. And if a woman turned down a male cadet, she was labeled a dyke. It was truly a no-win situation.

What made it worse was a tradition at the service academies in which nineteen-, twenty-, and twenty-one-year-olds had almost total power over eighteen-year-olds as part of a "leadership laboratory." At night and on weekends, the officers in charge went home and left the administration of the dorms to the second-, third-, and fourth-year cadets. Within this system, freshmen cadets lived in a constant "basic training" environment. They had to march everywhere, were frequently harangued and yelled at, and had to always obey the orders of any upperclassman.

The military teaches and trains us for the superior/subordinate relationship because it is fundamental and sacred to our mission. Subordinates must both trust their superiors and do what they are told, because lives are at stake. The superior, in turn, must be a good steward of this power and responsibility and be focused on the mission and the team. But there is significant potential for this power to be abused. And it was, over me and so many others.

An upper-class male cadet could order a first-year female cadet to report to his room, alone—and some male cadets did just that to me and also to many others. Failure to comply would open a female cadet up to harassment and hazing. In my case, the male cadet's intent was clear and made even clearer in his room.

At the time, some of the academy leadership failed to recognize that we lived in a rigid but frequently unsupervised, high-intensity, hierarchical environment, where despite bans on drinking in the dorms, there was drinking. It was legal on campus and in town to drink beer with a lower alcohol content at age eighteen. This was a bad combination, and it increased the likelihood for sexual assault and abuse of power.

I personally experienced episodes of degrading treatment during my four years. But I didn't expect to be degraded by my friends. That stung. During my senior year, a close friend indicated he was interested in starting a relationship with me. At an off-campus party, he added alcohol shots to my beer, then lured me to a separate room. As we kissed, he removed my shirt, and then on cue, his buddies (who up until that moment I thought were my friends as well) rushed in and snapped a photo of me. They all laughed as I scrambled to cover myself and leave. It was a preplanned ambush. The photo was shared with other guys in my squadron, who taunted me relentlessly. These were supposed to be my teammates, my trusted wingmen. I felt violated and betrayed, but I also felt I couldn't tell anyone. I spent the last four months of my senior year counting the days until graduation, with my superior officers asking me over and over again, Cadet McSally, where has your fire gone?

I wish I could say that these were merely isolated incidents, but for me and many other cadets in that time period, they added up to a disturbing pattern.

At one point early in my Air Force experience, I had a senior officer prey upon me, much as my high school track coach had done. I almost started to think this was how things worked and was simply what happened when a man in authority "valued" a female underling. This is the corrosive, destructive thinking that traps many abuse victims, outside the military as well.

My high school experience with the abusive track coach had taught me that the easiest way to survive was to mentally "check out" when I found myself powerless in these circumstances. Military training also strengthened my ability to compartmentalize and disassociate, so I could function under high demands even after enduring abuse and assault. I remember rationalizing to myself that if it wasn't happening to me right now at this moment, it had no power over me.

If only that were true.

Years later, I decided I would confront this senior officer in private when I saw him again at another base. It was after work, on a Friday night. His response was to hold me down and rape me. I got to a safe place and spent the weekend curled up in the fetal position in shock. I told one friend, but we never considered reporting the crime. On Monday morning, I showed up to work on my base and even took a phone call from my rapist, where he acknowledged that he had raped me and apologized. I hung up the phone, walked to the tarmac, and flew my next mission, completely numb and emotionally dead. I thought it showed how strong I was, which was true to some degree, but it also meant I was not truly facing what I had endured and survived. I dedicated myself to excellence as an officer, pilot, and athlete, all the while keeping these horrific experiences locked away in the dark to fester and rot.

I have military friends who also experienced sexual harassment, assaults, and rapes but never reported them. We didn't trust the system or anyone in the chain of command to believe us or to do anything about it. We endured it, determined to survive and get on with our careers and lives.

Sex and sexual abuse are also more complicated in the overall military environment. Indeed, the issues in the active-duty military are even more fraught than in the service academies. What might in other circumstances look like two consenting adults in an intimate relationship has a very different dynamic when it involves superiors and subordinates. The military chain of command is a unique hierarchy: a superior can order you into battle, put you in jail, take away your money, and order you to do many things you would prefer not to do. If a superior crosses the line, a subordinate can feel compelled to do things that she or he—because many men are victims, too—would refuse to agree to in any other setting. Once I became a more senior officer, I realized this isn't sexual abuse of power, this is sexual assault. Within the unique and powerful superior-subordinate construct created by the military, a subordinate is in no position to "consent" to anything with a superior.

IT WASN'T UNTIL THE MID-NINETIES, while transitioning into being an attack pilot, that I decided to truly face all that I had survived and the impact it had on me. I was attending chapel services on my base in Arizona and got involved with a faith-based young-adult group. I heard stories from friends who had also been abused and made the courageous choice to discuss their horrific experiences and begin to heal. As I listened to them explain the dynamics of how it impacted their lives, everything sounded so familiar. I realized that all my compartmentalization, rather than making me powerful, had rendered me emotionally dead. I was not allowing anyone, not myself, not even God, into those dark corners of my life.

One of the most helpful things I did was to read a stirring book titled *The Wounded Heart* by Dan Allender and attend one of his seminars. I acknowledged to myself and others for the first time that I was also living with the deep wounds of sexual abuse and assault. At last, things began to make sense to me. I started on the tumultuous but wonderful journey toward healing, with the help of trusted wingmen. Indeed, one of them was the man I would briefly marry, who was incredibly supportive and a true blessing as I faced these awful truths. I also worked closely with a caring mentor in the ministry.

What sustained me through all these difficult experiences was, and continues to be, God. My relationship with Him was critical to my ability to survive and thrive, even when I was not fully willing to open the closed doors inside my heart. By experiencing God's healing hand and being accepted as I am by people who truly loved me, I was able to walk the turbulent path toward softening my heart, trusting people again, and truly living, loving, and being loved.

For the first time, I told my family and close friends what I had survived. I also searched for ways to hold that predatory track coach accountable and prevent him from abusing other girls. Too much time had elapsed for criminal charges, which meant my only option was a civil lawsuit. But I wasn't damaged; I had succeeded in spite of his abuse, so I declined. As hard as it is to accept, there are limitations to seeking justice on this earth for these complex violations.

I was determined to thrive in and through the darkness, to not let my pain derail me, and somehow grow from these experiences—looking forward through the windshield, not focusing on the rearview mirror. And I did.

IN 2003, THE AIR FORCE Academy experienced significant scrutiny as sexual assault victims spoke out and demanded change. In the 2003 graduating class alone, 12 percent of women reported that they were victims of rape or attempted rape while at the academy. A staggering 70 percent reported having been victims of sexual harassment. The academy was under pressure to reform its culture. I was selected to become a group commander at the school, no doubt to help clean up the mess. But I felt as if the Air Force wanted me as a public relations tool to distract the media and public, so that the top brass could say, "Look, here is a successful female academy graduate who became our first woman to fly in combat. Not all women were assaulted here." Like many of the women now coming forward, I had stayed silent and had not shared my own horrific experiences. Internally, I struggled with my obligation as a leader and an officer. I did not want to negate my experiences, but I also recognized that they were in the past. The best thing I could do in this moment was to help the academy and the entire Air Force change their culture. Above all, I very much wanted to do what was best for the Air Force.

I met with my commander to discuss the general situation without sharing any personal details. I also decided to reach out to a good friend who was a senior lawyer with the Air Force's Judge Advocate General (JAG) and also a person whom I really trusted and still do. Launching investigations for crimes committed many years prior would never lead to charges, due to the statute of limitations and the difficulty of proving them. So, I didn't want to take that path. I wanted to look to the future and help the Air Force find ways to protect other military women and men.

I called my friend at home, off duty, and walked him through each of my experiences, asking what he thought would be the most constructive way for me to share them to help the Air Force that we both served in and loved. Like me, my friend was concerned that if I provided specific details about what I had survived, the Air Force would decide to apply the letter of the law, state that I had just reported sexual assault, and initiate criminal investigations.

Complicating my decision was the reappearance of that former upperclassman who had abused his power over me in the dorms while I was a cadet. He was now married, a father, and a successful officer. Although I felt as healed as I will be this side of heaven from all I endured, I was still a little rattled by the prospect of having to interact with him again, as a subordinate. Accelerant was poured on this concern when he was asked to introduce several of us at a public event. When he got to me, he said something like: "And last but not least, we have Lieutenant Colonel McSally, who I have known since she was a sweet young cadet at the Air Force Academy." Everyone else chuckled, not understanding the deep, smug cruelty of the remark. I was enraged. It was like listening to an uncle who has molested a niece pointing out how cute she is at a family gathering. No one but the victimized child grasps the meaning of what the abuser is saying, but it subtly continues the dynamics of abuse.

I got through the event without screaming, crying, or decking him, all definite possibilities. I called my lawyer friend and also spoke with another close friend. They both agreed that I had very limited legal options for any response. After much contemplation and prayer, I came up with a plan. I decided to confront the former upperclassman, enter information about all of my experiences on the anonymous military sexual assault survey sent to all women in the Air Force, and be ready to honestly answer any media questions, acknowledging in general that I was also an assault survivor without kicking off fruitless investigations.

Using my work computer, I wrote an email to my JAG friend's work email account. I laid out my general plans, and I used the words "rape" and "sexual assault/abuse" in the email. I also found the courage to confront the former upperclassman, which was harder than flying in combat. He admitted his wrongdoing, asked for forgiveness, told me how courageous it was for me to confront him (which in truth only angered me more), and then it was over. I felt as if I had taken back the power that he had held over me.

I never learned exactly what transpired next, but soon after, following a night training flight, I was awoken early by a call from my JAG friend. He said he was being questioned regarding what he knew about my sexual assault and other experiences. He had refused to say anything without my permission, but asked if he could share what I had told him. Confused and shocked, I said yes. What was going on? Had the words "rape" and "assault" in my message tripped off an alert in the military email system, which is monitored by the government?

Months later, after I was selected to be an A-10 squadron commander (and consequently was not sent to the Air Force Academy), I was asked to speak with the Air Force Inspector General's office regarding an ongoing, unrelated investigation in which I was a witness. I walked into the room prepared to discuss what I knew, and instead, the investigators produced a copy of the email I had sent my JAG friend, shoved it in front of me, and demanded that I explain the details of my sexual assaults.

My mind screamed, What??? All I could think was, Is this the way the Air Force treats sexual assault victims? They spoke to me as if I were the criminal, trying to pressure me to confess details of the crimes I had been a victim of, so they could fully investigate them.

I was horrified. First, I couldn't believe this was how officials handled unreported crimes. Second, anyone with a knowledge of sexual assault understands that asking a victim to retell their story, even decades later, can be a traumatic experience. Even though I was a successful officer and fighter squadron commander, they had no business treating me so callously. Third, they spoke in a bullying tone, as if *I* had done something wrong, trying to pressure me to "do your duty as an officer" and disclose the crimes committed against me. This is the classic revictimization that often occurs when assault allegations are handled by people who lack an understanding of how to appropriately and compassionately deal with victims.

Disgusted, I replied that I was not going to tell them anything, and that if I had felt safe and comfortable telling Air Force officials about the assaults, I would have done so at the time. They were demonstrating exactly why I and many other women and men simply didn't trust the system. I berated them for being so unskilled and ignorant. It wasn't G-rated. I left feeling angry and dismayed, thinking it was over, but it wasn't.

My JAG friend then told me that he was now being investigated for giving me private advice. This was unbelievable. Months later, while I was deployed to Afghanistan, I received an email from him that the Air Force had finished its investigation had concluded that he should not have offered me any advice and instead should have referred me to defense counsel regarding "possible" *crimes that I had committed*! He would face repercussions for having tried to help me. Imagine this—I reached out to him initially, and he gave me advice—for the betterment of the Air Force we both loved. As a result, now we were both being accused of wrongdoing!

The Air Force investigator also concluded that, as a subordinate, it was MY responsibility to maintain "professional relationships" with my superiors and I had behaved "unprofessionally" by allowing "sexual activity" to take place between a superior officer and me. (This was the same superior officer who had preyed upon me and later raped me.)

And people wonder why the military has a problem dealing with sexual assault.

This was far worse than the incompetent investigators demanding I tell them details of the crimes I had survived. Even more appalling, this Air Force investigator had reached his conclusions without ever speaking to me. I was enraged. I sent an email to the secretary of the Air Force, a civilian, and the chief of staff of the Air Force, General Moseley, the same general who had been my boss and who had encouraged me to wear the abaya one time. I told them I was going to my congressman, then the media, if they didn't resolve this unconscionable situation immediately. This was a clear case of some people in senior positions blaming the victim on paper (not just privately among themselves) for being abused or raped. The basic subject line of my email, Being raped all over again, got their attention.

I can't fully express how devastated I was that the Air Force I loved was screwing this up so badly. I was a deployed A-10 commander in a war zone, who needed to focus all my energy on the mission. And now this crap was landing in my email inbox. I took a long walk around the base, eventually stopping in the chapel to pray and ask God for strength and wisdom. Although it was the middle of the night in Washington, D.C., in a few hours I received an email reply from General Moseley saying he was looking into it and would get back to me very soon. Looking back after we both had retired, he described the entire situation as "flawed process, indefensible investigative actions," and "just a lack of ethically/legally sustainable actions."

Within a few days, I received a full letter from him stating that he had reviewed the report and concluded that I had done nothing wrong. The "charges" against my JAG friend were dropped. The report was closed.

Very soon after, I received the news that I had been promoted to the rank of colonel and selected to attend the Air Force's war college. In return, I had to commit to spending another four years in uniform. In the Air Force, promotions at this level had become high pressure and draconian. If I did not want to accept the assignment to the Air War College, I would be terminating my career. Air Force policy stated that any form of a "no" would result in me being "separated" from the Air Force in ninety days, and, although I had served for eighteen years, I would forfeit my right to any benefits and retirement pay. Still, after the so-called investigation, I was ready to hang up my combat boots and wings. My wing commander prevailed on me to focus on completing my current deployment to Afghanistan, return home safely, reflect, and then make my decision. I have him and his thoughtful advice to thank for keeping me in the Air Force for four more years.

"WHY DIDN'T YOU REPORT HIM?" "Why didn't you immediately tell a superior?" These are not easy questions in any workplace, but especially in the military. Much as in a high-intensity civilian workplace, in the military, you spend long hours with your colleagues. But there are also vast differences. You frequently live with these colleagues on base or very close by, and your superior officers do not simply have power over your work life, they retain actual legal authority over you. In a "he said/she said" claim, any subordinate who comes forward is highly likely to be ostracized and damaged, both professionally and personally, and be accused of being "out for revenge." For too many years, sadly, the likelihood of bad outcomes was far higher if you reported an incident than if you kept your mouth shut. Now, the courage of individual women and men is changing that environment. But there is still more that needs to be done.

When I reached out to my JAG friend and later dealt with the Air Force investigators, there were no victims' advocates or special victims' counsels (SVCs), trained lawyers specifically offered to victims to advocate for them. Unlike many others, I was fortunate to have a trusted friend who was a JAG officer, and I remain eternally appreciative of his advice and support at such a critical time. Today there are well-resourced and protected SVCs. There is also counseling, which is a necessary form of help for many victims. Because of my distinctive experiences as both a commander in the Air Force and as a survivor, I believe I have a special responsibility to lead efforts to combat military sexual assault. It's an honor to be that unique voice in Congress. I told the world that I, too, was a sexual assault survivor in a Senate Armed Services Committee hearing. In 2019, seventeen of my eighteen legislative provisions on sexual assault in the military passed both houses and were signed into law.

For decades, the Air Force—and indeed much of our society—existed in a culture of disbelief. Many men and women didn't understand that there were actual predators in their squadrons; the assumption was always that it was happening somewhere far away, to someone else. Years later, a fellow officer and close friend said to me, "I realize now that there are far more of those men in our midst than I would have believed." He went on to say that this same complete lack of awareness and understanding "was and is fully present in our investigators. It's about perspective, and we don't have it. I believe that very, very many *good and decent men* still do not understand this at all."

BACK IN THE NINETIES, I took a long drive in Texas after being raped, and I listened to a song called "Seventy Times Seven" by David Meece (years later, we met and became friends, and he sang at my squadron change-of-command ceremony). The lyrics spoke of forgiveness and forgiving others just as God forgives us of all our transgressions, big and small. I played the tape over and over and over until I reached my destination. I knew God was calling me to forgive the officer who had raped me.

It is important not to conflate forgiveness with reconciliation, because they are very different. Forgiveness is letting go of the offense and not letting it have any power over you anymore. Reconciliation is a restoration of the relationship. We are called to forgive, and we are freed when we forgive, but we are not necessarily called to reconcile with the other person.

Forgiveness may be conveyed to the person who hurt you, but it doesn't have to be. Most importantly, it is a change in your own heart, where you free yourself. The only people who are hurt by "unforgiveness" are you and those around you—not the perpetrator. The Christian writer Joanna Weaver has written, "Bitterness is the poison you swallow expecting the other person to die." In fact, when we as victims toss and turn at night with the turmoil and anger of what we experienced, you can be sure your attacker or abuser isn't losing sleep thinking about you.

With the grace of God leading me, I was able to come to a true place of forgiveness, freed from the rage and sense of betrayal—feelings that were punishing me, not the man who assaulted me.

It took me much, much longer, however, to forgive my track coach.

HAVE YOU EVER GOTTEN UP to go to the bathroom in the middle of the night and tripped on something left on the floor or run into a piece of furniture after miscalculating its location? Then you reach for the light switch and voilà, you have perfect situational awareness of all the obstacles and the pathway.

In life's journey, you can't necessarily drown out all the darkness, but you can make choices and embrace concrete ways to turn a light on in the darkness. I once read a line in a book: "Feelings that are buried are buried alive." I believe it is true, because I lived it. We all have the option of trying to hide horrible, tragic, and shameful experiences in the dark forever. The problem is, just because they are hidden in the darkness, that does not mean that they have vanished. They still impact your life, your choices, and your future. But if you are able to bring those experiences into the light, they can be acknowledged, and the wounds can begin to be healed by God's grace. The process you choose to turn on the light, whether sharing with a trusted friend or loved one, counseling, or another route, is up to you. The key is to shine a light on the wound. Yes, you will have scars, but they will be a reminder of the healing and not the injury.

Shining a light on my painful experiences was healing in itself. I felt as if I could breathe again. I didn't have to use my energy to hide or bury my emotions. I allowed God to heal the wounds and restore my heart to truly live and love as He designed.

Understanding the deep wounds that came from the abuse and assaults I experienced helped me to see that I had protected my heart and lived much of life with my head—it was safer and more rational. Shining a light on what I had survived helped me to better understand myself, my relationships, my fears, and the patterns I used to protect myself. After facing my experiences, I, and those who know and love me, could identify those patterns and give me the chance to make different and healthier choices.

I can honestly say that I am stronger, more capable, and better able to love deeply today because of the entirety of my life experiences, including the tragic and painful ones.

I titled this chapter "Thrive Through the Darkness" because life on this earth can be filled with darkness, and, even with the right attitude and choices, fears and hurts don't disappear completely. Still, it is possible to live and thrive through the darkness, trusting that the darkness can't last forever and that the night will end.

In the Old Testament story of Joseph, after he is thrown into a pit, sold into slavery, jailed, and eventually rises to a position of leadership, he says, "What others intended for evil, God used for good." I believe those words with all my heart. I am a survivor of sexual harassment, abuse, and assault. It is a part of my life journey. It doesn't define me, but I will not pretend that it didn't happen. I can now say, though, that like Joseph, I have used my experiences for good.

In whatever struggles and darkness you may face, I hope that you can find a way to do the same.

ELEVEN

Trust Your Wingmen

"The power of two enables many
of us to continue to fight, in all
aspects of life."

A-10 ATTACK PILOTS DON'T FLY solo. Even though we sit in the cockpit alone, we travel in formations of two or four. Each pilot has a role. There is always a flight lead, the more experienced and capable pilot, who is responsible for decisions and tactics, and a wingman, whose job is to "look out" for the flight lead. (There is an old pilot joke that a wingman should only say three things on the radio: "Bingo" for low fuel, "Mayday," the emergency call prior to ejecting, and, "Lead, you are on fire.")

Concentrating on maps, the ground, and the target, the lead is vulnerable if an enemy opens fire. The wingman is tasked with keeping watch and keeping them both alive. We all need wingmen in our lives—to look out for us and to give us mutual support. The best wingman stays in position and knows where to look, and when. A good wingman recognizes how to prioritize tasks, what to say on the radio, and when to point out threats. Leads and wingmen prefer to fly in "combat pairs," and over time, the trust we build becomes second nature.

The power of two (or more) has an extraordinary dynamic. In the military, we train in groups; we face danger in groups. Those experienced in war understand that individuals will not survive long alone on the battlefield. Fear easily withers human will and strength. But the presence of a fellow comrade-in-arms fighting alongside changes everything. My success in that challenging Afghanistan canyon mission did not arise solely from my ability to do things afraid. It came from everyone whoever had faith in me, and from knowing that I had a controller on the ground and a wingman who had my back.

The power of two enables many of us to continue to fight, in all aspects of life. Having another soldier at your shoulder, another airman on your wing, or another hand in the darkness makes all the difference.

I have been blessed to have had many amazing wingmen in my life, too many to list. I couldn't have done what I share in this book without them. To succeed during pilot training, our class of students studied together, quizzed each other, and encouraged each other before evaluations. When I was fighting the abaya battle, feeling isolated and worn down, my friend Chaplain Katherine Shindel started emailing me daily words of encouragement that kept me going. And who knows what would have happened if then–Colonel Lawrence Stutzriem had not been posted to Saudi Arabia and been willing to take a fresh look at that outrageous policy toward American servicewomen, giving me hope to keep fighting.

Some of my most important wingmen while I was finding my way in the Air Force were women—specifically, female World War II pilots. When I was a fairly new A-10 pilot, I joined an organization called the Daedalians, a fraternity of military pilots. Most members were World War II, Korean War, and Vietnam War pilots, and I deeply appreciated their inspiring stories and friendship. But, like my other mentors, they were all men. At the monthly meetings, I was usually the only woman in the room. Until one lunch meeting, when three older women sat at my table and introduced themselves as World War II Women Airforce Service Pilots.

I am sure I had heard of women flying in World War II, but I had never met any of these amazing pioneers.

Some eleven hundred women served as pilots, in which capacity they not only trained male pilots, but also towed targets behind their planes to train gunners on the ground, ferried aircraft, and performed other missions. They wore uniforms, marched, and went through the same training as the men, but Congress refused to grant them military status. Thirty-eight died in the line of duty, and in a number of cases, their fellow pilots chipped in their own money to pay to have these women's remains returned to their families because the military did not.

After the war, these extraordinary trailblazers were sent home with no medals or veteran status. Finally, in 1977, they were retroactively awarded veterans' status and the right to a burial with full military honors at all veterans' cemeteries—receiving the medals they had earned required another act of Congress in 1984. But when I met these three feisty pilots in the mid-nineties, they still weren't allowed to join the Daedalians.

Dawn Seymour, Eleanor Gunderson, and Ruth Helm

were the wingwomen I needed. I loved listening to their crazy stories of training and flying. They were patriotic, gutsy, funny, and proud of their years of service. When I was enduring a lot of hostility and feeling discouraged, a dinner with these women would lift me up and give me perspective. When I contemplated leaving the Air Force a few times, they would look at me funny and ask, "Why would you give it up?"

When I was selected as the first woman in U.S. history to command a fighter squadron, they sat in the front row at my ceremony, in their uniforms, and beamed with pride. They gave me a set of custom glasses, engraved with their wings and the words WASP WWII. I use those glasses for special occasions and cherish my memories of my precious times with these heroes. Dawn, Eleanor, and Ruth have all passed away, but their legacy continues.

When I arrived in Congress, I finally had an opportunity to become their wingwoman. In late 2015, the media reported on a World War II female pilot named Elaine Harmon, who was denied burial at Arlington National Cemetery. Apparently, some lawyers or bureaucrats had decided that the 1977 law only applied to cemeteries run by the Veterans Administration. Arlington was managed by the Army, so, even though other female World War II pilots had been laid to rest there, it quietly rescinded the right. In a handwritten letter, Elaine had asked for a place at Arlington, and her family refused to accept the Army's denial.

I was shocked and infuriated. Very few female pilots of

that era were even still alive. How, more than seventy years after the war ended, could these pioneers be told that they counted for less than the men who performed the same missions?

The Army dug in, saying that it lacked the authority to make the change without an act of Congress. Given the level of dysfunction in D.C., that would normally be a depressing thought. But I led the effort to pass legislation in the House and Senate and have it signed into law. Later that year, I was honored to attend Elaine Harmon's funeral at Arlington with her family, friends, and other female pilots. It has been one of the most meaningful moments of my time "deployed" to D.C.

SOMETIMES, YOUR WINGMEN GIVE YOU cover just by showing up, as I learned with my housemates as a pilot-trainee in Arizona.

When I was in graduate school at Harvard, I volunteered at a neighborhood soup kitchen through my church. In addition to serving food, we sat and talked to those who came to eat. Unfortunately, one of the regulars started following me back to my apartment and then showing up at church services. Soon, he was stalking me. He would sneak into my apartment building or call the operator, claim an emergency, and break into our phone line when my roommates or I were on a call. He was obsessive and threatening. Once, when I got into my pickup truck and began to back out of my apartment's parking garage, he reared up in the back of the covered cab. I screamed, and he told me to keep driving. I wasn't sure if he had a weapon, but I felt as if I was being held hostage. For hours, I drove my truck around greater Boston as I tried to reason with him. I finally convinced him to let me drop him off at a hospital. I went to the police but was told that I couldn't get a restraining order because we weren't married and he hadn't yet hurt me physically. I spent the last several weeks of my time in grad school on my guard and not going anywhere alone. Harvard's graduation was held outdoors, and I was worried the whole time, scanning the area, in case my stalker showed up.

This unease followed me to pilot training, and at first, I lived in the bachelors' officer quarters because I was concerned for my personal safety. But I really wanted to live off base, which provided a better quality of life. Finally, I decided to move to a rental house with two pilot-training classmates. Because I was only one of two females in pilot training, they were men. But it was like having two more brothers. I felt safe in a home with my two wingmen, even if they did tend to leave their dirty dishes in the sink.

THE WINGMEN IN OUR LIVES don't have to come in uniform. In fact, they don't even have to have two feet. In their own way, some of my best wingmen in life have had four paws. Not only have the four-pawed kind brought joy into my life, but they've also found some wonderful human wingmen for me, too.

As soon as I received my first steady Air Force assignment as an instructor pilot, I adopted Bennigan, a golden retriever, followed by Penelope (another golden, who mostly annoyed Bennigan in her last year). Penelope lived an extraordinary life. In Germany, where I was stationed and then worked, dogs are allowed in restaurants, on trains, and in cable cars, and Penelope went everywhere with me. She had her own "dog passport" and traveled to eleven countries!

Serving in the military makes it challenging to care for a dog. The hours are long and irregular and there are frequent deployments overseas. I couldn't have had my dogs without sitters, walkers, friends, and family. After 9/11, I drove Bennigan back and forth across the country to my brother's house in Rhode Island five times in sixteen months, so his family could care for her while I was sent to the Middle East.

It was Penelope who brought me close to two precious humans, my next-door neighbors in Arizona, Phil and Helene, who became like family to me. Phil was a Navy vet who then worked mostly in commercial refrigeration, but he had retired early with health issues. I would see Phil and Helene and say hi when getting the mail or coming back from a walk. We had a cordial, neighborly relationship. Then Penelope arrived.

When Penelope was still a puppy, she would exit through

the doggy door into the backyard early in the morning. Phil was usually feeding the hummingbirds or tinkering in the yard. His heart melted for Penelope and he started inviting her into his yard to play. The first time it happened, I couldn't find Penelope anywhere. After my initial panic, I heard Phil and Penelope, and I knew it was mutual love. After Bennigan died, Penelope spent her days with Phil while I was at work on base. When my deployment orders to Afghanistan came, Phil and Helene insisted that Penelope stay with them.

Phil wanted to bring her to the base to greet me when I returned, but he was concerned how Penelope would react to the loud jet noise. So, after I left, he would walk her by the railroad tracks close to our home to help desensitize her. It was awesome to pull my jet into its parking spot after a long deployment and see Penelope waiting for me with Phil and Helene. I greeted the three of them before I greeted my commander!

When I was in Germany with Penelope, Phil and Helene became a volunteer foster family for our local golden retriever rescue, caring for goldens who were abandoned or neglected. One big old golden was named Rudy, and he had cancer. Rudy was afraid of thunder, and the only thing that would comfort him was driving around in a vehicle. Whenever a storm came, Phil would load Rudy into a van and drive him around until the storms subsided, even if it took all night. You can learn a lot about people by the way they care for animals.

In April 2014, Penelope passed away from a rare cancer, and Phil and Helene were with me as we said goodbye to her. She was as much their dog as mine.

Every time I have lost a dog it has been heartbreaking, but I cannot live my life without a dog. We don't replace our furry friends who pass on, we add to the family with new members and continue to love as we move forward. Rescue a Golden of Arizona called me the Thursday before Memorial Day weekend asking if I could accept a rambunctious, high-energy, ten-month-old male. Boomer joined me (and Phil and Helene) the next day. In his previous home, we were told Boomer was left outside and used the swimming pool as a water bowl. He had eaten kibble straight out of the bag and hadn't learned to socialize with people or dogs, so we had a steep learning curve. He would stick his whole head in his water bowl and slobber up the water, pushing half of it out onto the floor. When I first put his food in an aluminum bowl, he would eat some of it, then pick up the bowl, run into the living room, and spin in circles, flinging the kibble like a cluster bomb.

Boomer is also a thief. He steals things and takes them outside in the backyard to bury—hats, shoes, clothes, you name it. He is a professional digger. He uses his nose and paws to push the dirt over his buried treasure, leaving no indication that the earth has been disturbed. Phil's favorite hat was missing for months until Boomer finally dug it up. When my mom visited, her pajamas went missing for weeks. We finally found them—top, bottom, and socks—rolled up and buried behind Phil and Helene's mesquite tree. Boomer makes me laugh all the time. His mischievous personality can brighten up any day.

Boomer thinks it is normal to live in two houses. We used to have a hole in the wall for Penelope to easily go back and forth. Now we have a gate so the humans can access both yards, too. Boomer has doggy doors in both houses and food bowls as well. A few times he has been served two meals. He used to sneak out very early and head next door for breakfast, then tiptoe back to my room and pretend he was getting up for the first time—and starving—when I woke up!

For eighteen months, we continued our happy, two-household ritual, until Phil had a series of devastating health events including a serious oral cancer diagnosis. He pulled out of the immediate crisis, but the worst was in front of him. Phil had become like a second father to me, so I found myself in the role of many adults, being an advocate and a caregiver. Phil needed a feeding tube, complex surgery, radiation, and chemotherapy, resulting in multiple ER visits, during which we almost lost him from the side effects of the treatment. He endured long stays in the hospital and much suffering. Helene was trying to balance a full-time job and caregiving, and I would often fly home from D.C. and go straight to the VA hospital to be with Phil. Boomer was allowed to visit as well, and that was a blessing for both of them.

In May of 2017, the VA doctor called me in D.C. and told me to get on the next plane because he sensed Phil had reached the end of his life. It is a long trip, changing planes, from D.C. to Tucson. When I arrived, Phil was unconscious but still alive. We stayed with him through the night. The next day, Helene and I were there. Boomer lay at the foot of Phil's bed, with his head often resting on Phil's leg. It was precious and heartbreaking. Phil's breathing was labored, and it appeared that he was fighting to stay. We called a close friend in the ministry, and he prayed over Phil with us on speakerphone, asking God to peacefully take his spirit and telling Phil it was okay to let go, that we would take care of Helene. During the prayer, Phil's breathing eased, and he took his last breath as God took his spirit home.

Boomer, Helene, and I remain blessed to have each other, right next door.

None of us knows where we will find the wingmen in our lives. They might sit down next to us at a lunch table, as those female pilots did. They might move in next door or come as allies in animal rescue. They could be someone you once teased in school—or who teased you. Or they might be as brief a presence as that air strike controller on the ground in Afghanistan and my pilot wingman in the air. Some of my fellow pilots, who initially resisted women flyers, over time became both amazing friends and sources of support. What they all have in common is they need to be worthy of your trust, and you of theirs, because no matter what task we embark on, none of us is truly alone.

When you have an opportunity to become someone else's wingman, take it. It can make all the difference for you both.

TWELVE

Get to the Next Water Station

"The difference between victory or defeat often lies in your head."

I BELIEVE THAT ANYONE WHO doesn't have a major health issue can cross the finish line of a marathon. As long as they follow a training plan, invest in the right running shoes, and stay injury-free, their body can traverse 26.2 miles. I also believe that the vast majority of people who do none of these things, but still decide to stand at the starting line to see if they can conquer the course, will fail.

I don't just believe this, I know it to be true. Over the years, I coached a number of people to complete their first marathon. But when I commanded an A-10 squadron in Afghanistan, I said it to some members of my team and a number of them balked. They were sure they could not run a marathon, and some did struggle to complete the 1.5-mile run on the annual Air Force fitness test. So, I challenged them to let me prove it—using them as my proof. I would come up with a training plan, we would all follow it as a group, and together we would run the San Diego Marathon. They agreed.

A marathon is one of the most challenging races to train for because of the psychological element. And it is only one component of an Ironman triathlon, which combines a 2.4-mile swim, a 112-mile bike ride, and a full, 26.2-mile marathon all in one day. So, of course, what was I determined to complete? An Ironman. And what Ironman did I want to finish? The Hawaii Ironman, known for being one of the toughest courses in the world. I had watched this race on television when I was an Air Force cadet and decided I would cross the finish line someday.

But I couldn't start in Hawaii. My first triathlon was a short one in Colorado, where I had to buy a bike and ride it for the first time in the race—something I wouldn't advise. I started running marathons only because I wanted to get enough of them under my belt to physically and mentally build up to the Ironman. My triathlon performance took off when I was in graduate school and trained with the Harvard cycling team, finally learning how to bike competitively. During grad school, I was assigned to the NATO political headquarters in Brussels, Belgium, for two summers. On weekends, I traveled to small villages around Belgium and even other countries to compete in triathlons. While registering for a race in July 1990, I saw a sign-up for an Ironman Triathlon in Middelkerke, Belgium. In my mind, this was just what I needed, even though I wasn't training for an Ironman at that point. I was twenty-four years old and about to head back to the U.S. to start pilot training, and was worried that my dream to complete an Ironman would take a back seat to my flight training. I signed up for the Middelkerke Ironman, and then began my "small" triathlon.

The swim came first. I was in the front group, going strong and fast. It's easy to lose track of time and distance in open waters. I remember seeing a buoy marked 500 METERS, which I thought meant we had completed the first five hundred meters of the fifteen-hundred-meter swim. Instead, we had only five hundred meters to go. But I wasn't looking for the finish line. Just beyond the marker, a man started swimming alongside me on the right. I was breathing to my right and he was breathing to his left, so we faced each other as we raced. I was determined not to allow him to pass me, so I did not pick my head up to look to the front. That proved to be a painful mistake.

The next thing I knew, I had crashed into something hard, headfirst. I was startled and confused by the impact. I finally raised my head and saw my fellow racer climbing onto a metal dock. I grabbed onto what I realized was the metal ladder I had rammed. Now I needed to jog up the trail to the bike area. As I pulled off my bathing cap, blood poured down my face from a gash in my head. An alarmed race official stopped me and yelled at me in Flemish, but I had no idea what he was saying. I pulled away and started jogging to my bike.

This was a major race. I was in the lead group of swimmers and was the first woman. I remember a helicopter overhead filming the race and announcing my name and country on a megaphone as I ran along the spectator-lined trail. People looked shocked as I passed. I remember thinking, Haven't they seen a woman keep up with the men before? I didn't understand that their shock was a response to the blood streaming down my face and body.

I reached my bike and wiped my face. There was a considerable amount of blood on my hand. I recalled from my premed studies that head injuries always bleed a lot and can look worse than they are. With adrenaline pumping and the clock running, I decided to put on my bike helmet to stop the bleeding. I wasn't in pain and figured I could be bandaged after I won and collected my trophy and the prize money.

As I lifted my bike off the rack, another race official grabbed my shoulders and spoke sternly to me in Flemish. I told him I was fine and to get his hands off of me, that he was slowing down my time. Yet another man joined him, trying to pull my bicycle away. He also grabbed me firmly by the shoulders, looked into my eyes, and stated in English: "You must stop, you are losing too much blood."

I relented, and they led me to the medical area, as I explained that I was fine. Suddenly, I started to gray out and lose my balance. The adrenaline was wearing off, replaced by the consequences of the hard hit and blood loss. Had they not insisted on stopping me, I would likely have passed out while riding my bike and crashed. Thank God for pushy Belgian men!

I had two things on my mind as the medics evaluated me. I had that Ironman in two weeks. And I didn't want them to shave my head (I had my priorities as a young woman). At the hospital, every time someone came toward me with a razor, I pushed them away, saying, please don't shave my hair. I eventually relented and was stitched up. I also told everyone I had an Ironman in two weeks. Finally, the doctor said bluntly, "No Ironman for you. You are finished." Finished? What did he know?

Two weeks later, I was in Middelkerke.

Middelkerke is on the northern Belgian coast and the swim would be in open water, into the cold, rough English Channel. Growing up on the ocean in Rhode Island, I was very comfortable swimming in open waters with waves and currents. Many triathletes learn to swim in a pool under controlled conditions. Rough waves and hard currents could unnerve them, but I saw them as a competitive advantage for me. My plan was to take it easy in the swim. Save my legs for the bike and run.

That day, the waves and currents were horrendous, and it was impossible to take anything easy. In the chaotic, choppy seas, I kept sucking in salt water instead of air, and coughing it up as I pushed forward. Several swimmers were pulled from the water. It was brutal. It is the only time I have felt nervous in water, and I hate to admit it, but I almost panicked. I didn't want to drown alone on the edge of the North Sea. My focus became getting to the shore alive.

I made it but was exhausted, my stomach and lungs burning from the salt water. I changed into cycling clothes, wondering how far I could go until I needed to stop. The bike section was a sixteen-mile loop that repeated seven times to reach the full 112 miles. When I signed up for the event, I thought this would help psychologically, breaking the race into achievable portions, but after the first two or three passes, it seemed like it would never end, and there was never any new scenery. Along the coast, the wind was stinging, about twenty to thirty miles an hour, which creates significant resistance. At ninety-seven miles, I got a flat tire and pulled off the road to repair it. I remember those moments clearly. I was thrilled that I only had fifteen miles to go, but then I realized I had been competing nonstop for almost seven hours, but still had to run a full 26.2-mile marathon that day! I couldn't fathom how my body would endure the remainder of this race. I should have listened to that Belgian doctor: "You are finished. No Ironman for you." I resigned myself. Lesson learned. I would run for a few miles and then head to my car.

The marathon course was ruthless. We ran parallel to the beach on a boardwalk, 2.6 miles out, then 2.6 miles back, ten times. I hadn't realized how demoralizing it would be to run across the finish line multiple times without being able to stop. I could overcome that with good compartmentalization and disassociation. But as on the bike, the wind was the will-breaker. It was a straight headwind on the way out, still ranging from twenty to thirty miles an hour, with blowing sand. For the return, the wind was at my back. The problem is I spent much more time in the headwind than in the tailwind, so in the misery-to-relief ratio, there was much more misery.

I convinced myself to put my shoes on and do one full lap and then return to Brussels. I put one foot in front of the other, as I did so many times in training and in other marathons. I leaned into the wind and turned my head to avoid inhaling sand and gutted my way to the turnaround. But once I turned, I had the wind at my back and hit a comfortable stride. I felt strong and convinced myself to do one more lap before I quit. On my way back on the second lap, I heard the announcer state that I was the only American in the race. I was in third or fourth place for the women (only twelve were crazy enough to enter, while there were 188 men).

Spectators starting yelling "Go America!" "Go American woman!" "Go U.S.A!" From thinking I could quit and sneak off, I was now representing my country. My patriotic duty drove me to turn around and plod into the sand and wind for a third time. The adrenaline from the national pride wore off pretty quickly, but I pushed forward, one step at a time. As I approached the turnaround, I started to talk myself into the belief that I *could* finish this Ironman. I had run 13.1 miles and only had 13.1 miles to go. It was all downhill from here! I had three more tailwind legs to go and only two more headwind legs. I tried to strengthen myself for the hard but achievable task ahead. I would intercept negative thoughts and replace them with: "Come on, you big baby, stop whining. You can do this. You just need to keep going. Don't quit. Don't give up. Lean into this and conquer it!"

I was running about a seven-minute mile on the tailwind and an eleven-minute mile on the headwind, so nearly twenty-nine minutes each way into the wall and only eighteen or so minutes with the wind pushing at my back.

Some friends from NATO headquarters came to cheer me on in the final stretch. I was determined to finish and decided that I wanted to break a four-hour time for the marathon. I crossed the finish line with a total time of eleven hours and forty-five minutes.

For the next several years, I continued to train, and, while I was a T-37 instructor pilot in Del Rio, I traveled to Germany to represent the United States at the world military triathlon championship. The day before, I was introduced to an American professional triathlete, whom I admired. She offered to let me use her bike. I thought a lighter, more expensive bike would help me. I adjusted the seat for my height and assumed it was good to go.

I was racing against some basically professional athletes from European countries who wore their military uniforms as a "job" while they trained for the Olympics or other elite sporting events. The woman favored to win had competed as a swimmer for France in the 1988 Olympics. I was working twelve hours a day, flying sometimes three times a day, as an instructor pilot and trying to fit in training on the side.

The race started in the afternoon. I emerged in second position behind the Olympian in the swim, hopped on my borrowed bike, and began the twenty-five-mile course. A few miles in, I heard something rattle in the handlebars. I ignored it. Soon, I could feel the handlebars loosen, and at one point, a part came off. I was mortified that this high-tech bike was starting to fall apart—and in my best part of the race. I held the handlebars together and made it to the run. I ended up in fourth place, just off the medal platform.

Back in the U.S., I set my sights on the Hawaii Ironman.

I was still working long hours as an instructor pilot. In hot summer months, with an old airplane and suboptimal air-conditioning, most pilots lost a few pounds in water weight and went home dehydrated after a day at work, which was five days a week. So, I did my long-distance bike training on Saturdays with a local cycling club. These guys, some from the base and others who lived in the community, were the best training partners. I wouldn't have achieved my athletic goals without them.

We worked our endurance up to one-hundred-mile Saturday bike rides, which could last five to six hours or more, depending on wind conditions. I would return home from the long rides, change my shoes, and go for a run. It is amazing how the human body can adapt and become stronger and faster with athletic training. The first time, I barely dragged myself to the end of my street and back for two miles. But each Saturday, I ran a little farther after the hundred-mile ride. Eventually, my longest brick workout— brick, because your muscles feel like bricks as you transition from biking to running—was a hundred-mile ride followed by a thirteen-mile run.

On Sundays, I would swim in the lake for a few miles, using my upper body while stretching my sore legs. I did my long-distance runs on Mondays. Eventually, I had my roommate drive me into work, and no matter how late or how tired I was, I ran the eighteen miles home. I had great wingmen during those runs. Some friends would start with me, some would meet me in the middle and run a section, and others would join me at the end and encourage me in the final, tiring miles.

Having people commit to joining me on the runs kept me accountable to complete them versus accepting a ride home and saying I was too tired. My mom also traveled to many of my races in the U.S., waiting near the finish line to cheer me on.

AFTER SO MANY HOURS IN the water, on the bike, and on the open road, I truly believe that the difference between victory and defeat often lies in your head. Many people give up under the extraordinary mental test. It does not help to stand at the starting line of a marathon and think about how long and painful it will be to get to mile twenty-five. Or to stand at the start of the Ironman and think about how you must power through the 112-mile bike ride after the arduous swim and then run a marathon. That is enough to make anyone turn around and go straight back to bed! Sometimes contemplating the size of the task can defeat us before we even start. It helps to view the path as achievable, not monumental. For example, I didn't start my first day of basic training and dwell on everything I would have to go through to graduate from the Air Force Academy four long, hard years later. On the first day of pilot training, I wasn't paralyzed by the difficulty, length, and magnitude of *all* the training, experience, and challenges I would need to navigate to become a fighter pilot four years later.

I have found that the best way to succeed at anything difficult is to focus on small, achievable milestones and complete them one at a time. For a marathon, the first milestone is the first water station. Usually these are placed every mile or maybe two. It is easy to focus on running a mile. With one mile down, it's time to get to mile two. Soon enough, you will reach the ten-mile marker. Slightly more than three miles later, you are halfway done and can enjoy the psychological boost of having less road in front of you than you have behind you.

Having reached that marker, I try to break the rest of the race into familiar chunks. I think of runs I did around my house: eight miles is the Saguaro National Park scenic loop (and the marathon is likely nowhere near as hilly as that run!); six miles is down to the railroad tracks and over to Houghton and back; four miles is the normal route that Boomer, my dog, and I take in the morning . . . you get the point. When you are tired, dehydrated, cramping, and want for it to be over, breaking the feat into doable chunks that are relatable to things you have already achieved helps you keep putting one foot in front of the other.

BY THE TIME THE HAWAII Ironman World Triathlon Championship arrived, I was trained and ready. The Hawaii Ironman was created by a U.S. naval officer and his wife in 1978, on Kona Island. The swim began with more than twelve hundred swimmers' flailing arms and legs (today, that number has risen to more than twenty-three hundred), following the tradition of "everyone start at once," then the bike ride, battling wind, hills, and heat from the lava landscape, and finally the marathon. But Hawaii seemed easy compared to Middelkerke, and it was for several reasons, including the conditions and my preparation. I was able to warm up and take it easy in the swim, minimizing the impact on my legs. I almost crashed at the beginning of the bike section when someone cut me off, but somehow I stayed upright. I felt fast and strong on the bike; I was on track to break ten hours and thirty minutes. Then I started on the run. My knee hurt and started to slow me down, but I was determined. The pain subsided or I got numb to it, and I slogged on through the lava fields. I remember running that final amazing stretch of Ali'i Drive as if it were yesterday.

There are many lonely miles on the Ironman course, but for the last section, it felt like the whole world was cheering me on. I was exhausted, dehydrated, and spent. For more than ten and a half hours, I had given my all. But I found a final burst of energy to sprint to the finish, crossing with a time of 10:45:00. I won the women's military division and placed twelfth in my age group in the world, not a bad showing for an amateur and someone who is not a naturally gifted athlete.

What led me to believe I could achieve these goals was not any faith in my talent, but my belief in the power of determination, discipline, training, milestone setting, perseverance, and possibly some good fortune along the way—which is why I believed that I could coach my squadron mates to run the San Diego Marathon—and they could succeed.

MOST MARATHON TRAINING PROGRAMS FOR beginners do not have them run the full 26.2 miles before the actual race. Unlike shorter races, where your training regimen includes "dress rehearsals" of the race distance, the marathon takes a substantial toll on the body and requires weeks of recovery. So, it is not smart for a beginner to run the 26.2 miles in training. Instead, the goal is to accomplish one long, slow distance run a week, peaking with a twenty- or twenty-two-mile run, one time.

The challenge for marathon rookies is to purposely slow down the long runs and to trust that they can finish a marathon. If you spend the whole training program mired in doubt and fear that you "might not" be able to finish a marathon, or be able to finish at your desired pace, then you ironically have a higher potential to overdo it and diminish your chances of success. To conquer the goal of running a marathon, you need to trust your training and follow it, putting aside any doubts. Doubt holds all of us back in countless situations other than marathon training. The more you focus on the doubt, the more likely you are to overdo preparation, make a mistake, or feel paralyzed and fail to accomplish the task. Instead, if you trust your training, you can stand at the starting line with confidence that you did everything necessary to succeed.

When my squadron returned from Afghanistan, we

kicked off our training program. Everyone was fitted for the right shoes, we did our long runs together, and we completed other runs during the week. I also made sure everyone was well nourished and well hydrated. I learned that lesson when I trained for a marathon in the 1990s with one of my friends. He started out thinking that not carrying water and not eating would somehow make the training more rigorous and more successful. But nothing could be further from the truth. I told him there are enough barriers and challenges in life, don't add more. Instead, set yourself up for success. Training, preparation, mental approach and, finally, execution. He ate and drank properly and finished two marathons.

The months passed quickly, and I told my squadron that we were ready. And we were. On race day, I ran back and forth to encourage them as they ran at different paces. I ended up logging close to thirty miles.

One of my marathoners, who earlier had struggled to pass the 1.5-mile Air Force fitness test and was the most skeptical about being able to finish, took it slow. But I knew he could do it—and I wanted him to believe it, too. I ran back to get him, and we crossed the finish line together. Our entire team was cheering him on as he reached a goal most people only dream about. That day, every one of my squadron mates crossed the finish line, and I was honored to run with them and encourage them, milestone by milestone. It was an extraordinary journey and accomplishment, and I am so proud of each of them, but especially my last finisher. In my book, he came in first.

THIRTEEN

Tap the Misery Database

"When we survive challenging
times, persevere through tragedy,
dig down deep to meet a difficult
goal, push through pain and
adversity, and succeed, it gives
us a memory to strengthen us
for future challenges."

WHILE I WAS SERVING WITH U.S. Africa Command, I decided to climb Mount Kilimanjaro in Tanzania with six friends and colleagues over Thanksgiving week in 2009. It was a grueling, six-day journey to reach the summit at 19,340 feet. One of my colleagues brought his twelve-year-old son. Twelve is usually too young, but his son was an elite runner, so he seemed prepared.

Kilimanjaro is not technically difficult, but it is physically challenging due to the altitude. You traverse through many ecosystems, starting with shorts in the rain forest and finishing wrapped in multiple layers for the freezing cold push to the beautiful glacier at the top. On our particular route, the success rate of making it to the summit was one-fourth to one-third of hikers.

The first day, we started at six thousand feet and finished at nine thousand. Day two took us from nine thousand to twelve thousand feet. For a pilot, losing supplemental oxygen above ten thousand feet is considered an emergency and requires an immediate descent. Now we would be choosing to spend several days in those conditions, so we needed to be smart about resting, hydrating, and eating well. Altitude sickness can hit anyone, regardless of their fitness, and it can be deadly. Everyone at these heights feels light-headed and winded and suffers from headaches, difficulty sleeping, and loss of appetite. Some will get nauseous and vomit. Those symptoms are mild and can be tolerated, but developing pulmonary or brain issues is often life-threatening.

We made it to twelve thousand feet, had a nice meal, and turned in for the night. For unknown reasons, I ended up having a horrible systemic allergic reaction, which caused my face to swell up, restricted my airway, and created turmoil in my gut. I was on a mountain far from medical help. I used an inhaler and took a Benadryl—I remember licking the crushed capsule out of the foil in desperation. I didn't want to wake my buddies, so I suffered quietly until the Benadryl kicked in. When the alarm sounded, my body felt awful, and I had gotten zero sleep. We set out on a day hike to acclimate our bodies to the altitude. To make it through, I leaned on my years of experience with sleep deprivation, endurance training, and misery tolerance—my misery database.

On day four, we hiked to a large communal hut located at fifteen thousand feet. For our final trek to the summit, we had to depart at midnight. Day five started in the cold and dark, and we needed to ascend another forty-three hundred, nearly vertical feet. We had planned our summit around a full moon to have moonlight illuminating our final push, but it was difficult to enjoy anything in these conditions. We wore headlamps and slowly crawled up the mountain in switchbacks, taking small, almost heel-to-toe steps to minimize exertion and sweating. We stopped every so often to rest, drink, and eat, but our guides told us that climbers who stop for long periods usually don't make it to the top. It felt like an eternity as we wound our way up that wretched mountain.

I had five layers on my top half and three on the bottom, double-layer mittens, a balaclava to keep my face warm, a hat, goggles, double-layered socks, and some gaiters to keep rocks and snow out of my boots and keep my calves and ankles warm. Even with all that, I struggled with being cold the whole way. I was also very nauseous. I would pull my balaclava off my face to expose my mouth to fresh air to help with the nausea. It would subside a little and be replaced by the despair of the cold. Then I would cover my mouth again and repeat the cycle. I hate being cold. It is one reason I fell in love with Arizona. I have a high tolerance for other pain and misery, but not cold. So here I was, spending my vacation time and money feeling awful and wishing God would turn up the temperature. But my misery was nothing compared to that of the twelve-year-old boy with us. He just wanted to quit.

At one stop, I tried to encourage him. I explained that we all wanted to quit. He was in better shape and had the benefit of youth. The rest of us were pushing ahead mainly by using mental skills we had developed over the years when we pushed through moments of misery and pain. I explained that we all have a misery database of life experiences. I was recalling basic training and flight training and combat, as well as running marathons and Ironman triathlons, and enduring deaths of family and friends. I was pulling all sorts of memories and experiences from my misery database, examples of the other times that I had pushed through and survived to strengthen and embolden me for this current challenge. I told him the problem was that even as a smart, talented, athletic twelve-year-old, his database was nearly empty. He was at a significant mental disadvantage compared to all of us in our forties and fifties, because he had few if any experiences to tell him that he could endure the pain and misery of this high-altitude trek. But right now, he was depositing a huge life experience in his misery database. If he could dig down deep and find the strength and courage to continue to put one foot in front of the other and make it to the summit, it would be an extraordinary experience and achievement. For the rest of his life, when he faced more difficult struggles or challenges, he could always reach back into his misery database and remember: "I climbed the highest mountain in Africa when I was twelve, so I can do this!"

He kept putting one foot in front of the other. He cried. He yelled at his father and us. He threw up. He stopped and declared he was finished. But ultimately, he made it to the top. Six years later, his parents sent me a video showing how he won a state high school track championship in the fifteen hundred meters, pulling far ahead of the entire field. I watched it as tears ran down my face. I knew he was reaching into his misery database and was running with the confidence of knowing that none of the other kids on the track had climbed Kilimanjaro at age twelve. It pushed him to become the champion.

The adage "what doesn't kill me makes me stronger" is true. (On the final day hiking down Kilimanjaro, I broke my kneecap and needed to follow my own advice—to tap into my misery database to complete the last ten miles while carrying my pack, which I stubbornly refused to give to one of the guys.) When we survive challenging times, persevere through tragedy, dig down deep to meet a difficult goal, push through pain and adversity, and succeed, it gives us a memory to strengthen us for future challenges. Adversity and difficulties viewed through this lens have positive potential in our lives. I have a pretty full misery database of challenges and I know many other people of character and rich experience who have much bigger ones than mine.

But there is one arena where it's particularly helpful to have a big misery database to draw upon, and that is politics.

MY JOURNEY FROM ACTIVE MILITARY duty to the halls of the U.S. Congress took nearly four and a half years. My last Air Force post was as chief of current operations at Africa Command, located in Stuttgart, Germany. Africa Command was a new organization, created from scratch, and I was part of the first leadership team, responsible for all U.S. military operations, emergency responses, and counterterrorism for the entire continent outside of Egypt. It was a high-stress, long-hour, fast-paced, and high-stakes job, and I gave it my all for three years. By summer 2010, I felt a strong inner conviction that it was time for me to move on to whatever my next mission was outside the military. I didn't have a plan for the next chapter, but I believe that sometimes each of us gets clarity on what we are no longer called to do before we find clarity on our next calling. I stepped out in faith, never imagining where that would lead.

My first stop was as a professor of national security studies at the George C. Marshall European Center for Security Studies in Garmisch, Germany, a little Bavarian town one hour south of Munich nestled amid breathtaking mountains and green pastures, with snowy winters. The Marshall Center was founded after the collapse of the Soviet Union to help newly free nations transition to democracy. Its students are diplomats, leaders, and emerging leaders in the military, police, intelligence services, or other organizations related to defense and security.

During my interview for the post, the dean asked, "Is there something about you that isn't reflected in your application package that you think we should know?" I answered, "I have a fire in my belly to make a difference in this world and I cannot put it out. It was lit in me as a young girl, when I lost my dad."

And it's true. I like to fix things that are broken and sometimes break things that are poorly built. The status quo is unacceptable to me. People and organizations are like any living organism: if you are not growing you are dying.

Being a professor at the Marshall Center is a dream job, and most people stay for at least five years. But just a year and a half after starting there, I pushed send on an email resigning my post. General Keith Dayton, my boss, replied three minutes later wishing me the best on my journey. There was no turning back. My next stop was as a candidate for Congress.

I had no political background or experience and had no clue what was required. Yet, as I sat in the stillness of that morning, I knew this was exactly what I was called to do for this season of my life.

Three elections and 1,041 days later, on December 17, 2014, after a mandatory recount, a judge declared me the winner in Arizona's second congressional district by a total of 167 votes.

Four years later, I gave up my House seat to run for the U.S. Senate and lost that race by another thin margin. As I was seeking my next mission, the governor of Arizona called and asked me to accept the appointment to serve in Arizona's other U.S. Senate seat, which former naval aviator and Vietnam POW John McCain had held until he passed away.

If I had let reason or risk aversion dictate my initial decision to run for Congress, all logic would have said don't do it. I am a middle-class military veteran with no connections to wealth or power and no elite status. And certainly, at the time, I had zero political experience. For much of my adult life, I was busy training or was deployed, and I voted absentee.

At the start of 2012, I didn't even have a house in Arizona to come home to—I had rented mine out while I was working in Germany. Very few people outside of my circle of friends knew my name. Yet I was ready to announce my candidacy to represent some seven hundred thousand people in southern Arizona. I wanted to serve in a new way and decided to act on it.

The irony is that for years, I was not remotely interested in "politics."

During my military career, friends and acquaintances repeatedly encouraged me to consider running for office someday, and the thought nauseated me. I do have a deep internal drive to not walk by a problem, to fix things that are broken and make things that are wrong right, to help those in need, and to see people reach their full potential. But like many in America, for a long time I had a general impression of politicians in D.C. as either incompetent or corrupt. But when I became a legislative fellow, serving in the office of Senator Jon Kyl, I began to reassess my views.

In fact, I sort of "blame" Senator Kyl, who represented Arizona, for my eventual decision years later to run for office, because he was a great example of a smart, hardworking man of character serving in the Senate as a workhorse and not a show horse. He was credible and well respected by both parties, and he had a knack for getting things done. Senator Kyl's example showed me that we had some good people of character in D.C., and more importantly that we *needed* more of them. But I didn't leave Senator Kyl's office wanting to run for office. Not even close. I loved making a difference on the public policy side, but still detested the politics of it all.

I certainly wasn't thinking about political office when I started at the Marshall Center. People save for years to vacation in a place like Garmisch, where the Center is located, and I had the chance to live and work there. Our day lasted from eight until five, which I used to joke was a half day compared to the hours I put in as a colonel in my final assignment. I had not experienced free time like this in years. I hiked every weekend, got my paragliding license, and often would go flying at lunch. I would change clothes, jump on the cable car less than a mile from the base entrance, lay out my glider, take off, fly over the mountains for fifteen to twenty-five minutes, pack up, change, and go back to work. What a life.

IT WAS LATE AT NIGHT in Germany on January 22, 2012, when I tuned in to watch the livestream of my home church in Tucson's annual event focused on starting the year off right. I felt stirred and blessed by the messages. I was starting to feel restless, like God was calling me to step out of my comfort zone, but I had no clue what that meant. I sat on my couch quietly for a few minutes after the session ended.

All of a sudden, news broke that my congresswoman, Gabby Giffords, was leaving Congress. The reason Gabby Giffords stepped aside was truly awful and heartbreaking. She was first elected in 2006, and on January 8, 2011, she was shot in the head by a deranged man in a devastating attack outside a grocery store that left six others dead and thirteen wounded. This mass shooting rocked our community, the city, and the country. It was a miracle that Gabby survived this horrendous assault, and her courage, grace, and perseverance during her long and difficult recovery and rehabilitation continue to inspire so many.

Her decision to retire would trigger an immediate special election. The primary would be held in roughly ninety days. The winner would serve for only six months and would have to stand for another election in November to win a full, two-year term.

Several of my colleagues and friends knew I was from Tucson. They sent me messages saying I should go home and run. When I passed my boss on the sidewalk, he even asked, "Hey, am I losing you?"

"No way," I replied. But by that night, my spirit was churning with the notion that I needed to consider stepping up to serve in a new way. I had moved to Arizona in the summer of 1990 to attend pilot training at Williams Air Force Base outside Phoenix, and despite the 115-degree summer temperatures, fell in love with the state and its beauty, people, and independent spirit. Four years later, I arrived in Tucson to train for the A-10 Warthog. I bought a home and hoped to stay as many years as possible. I was fortunate to have four assignments at Davis-Monthan Air Force Base, almost ten years of my twenty-two years of active duty.

I had a nine-day break before my next courses started. Maybe I could fly home to look into what it would take? While I was having dinner that night with a group of generals, I blurted out that I was thinking of heading home to run for Congress. Everyone at the table encouraged me to do it.

The next morning, I emailed Heather Wilson, the first female veteran elected to serve a full term in Congress, whom I came to know well during the abaya battle. She put me in touch with the chairman of the National Republican Congressional Committee. He gave me a tough-guy speech about what it takes to run. I needed to raise one hundred thousand dollars from my family and friends right away to show that people were willing to invest in me. I told him my family and friends did not have money to throw around, and I didn't take him totally seriously regarding the fundraising. I now know it is one of the most critical things you must do as a candidate because it is the only way to get your message out to the voters. I also knew I was going to have to make a very quick decision. I was still classified as a U.S. federal employee, and under the Hatch Act, no federal employee can "test the waters" for a political campaign without resigning.

I looked at the beautiful snowy Alps outside my window, and I wept, knowing in my spirit I was leaving for good. I would be following my calling, instead of my comfort. Thursday night, I called Senator Kyl. He told me he would set up appointments with people who could explain the political landscape and help inform my decision to run. (I later learned these meetings were intended to talk me out of it, something Senator Kyl and I laugh about often!)

By the time I landed in Arizona, I knew in my heart that

this was what I was called to do. I went to services at my local church and my pastor welcomed me home and asked me to lead a prayer. Afterward, an air traffic controller who had served with me when I was stationed at Davis-Monthan stopped to speak with me. He looked serious and said something like: "This is going to sound crazy, but as you were praying I got this very strong direction that I needed to come up here and tell you exactly what I used to say on the radio to you all the time at DM: 'Bulldog 01, runway 12, winds are 130 at 10, you are cleared for takeoff!'" I was speechless. I felt so encouraged by this and many other confirmations to step out in faith and run.

After resigning from my job, I met with Senator Kyl's southern Arizona staff, one of whom was already backing another candidate. For about two hours, they explained how I didn't have a chance in this race but would make a great candidate someday. "Don't waste your first political run on this election," was their message.

Finally, I said, "Hey, guys?"

"Yes, Martha?"

"I quit my job five hours ago."

"No! Can you get it back?"

"Maybe, but I don't want to. I am running for Congress." I said I had nothing to lose. They disagreed, adding I would come in a distant fourth place and would be labeled a political "loser." I laughed and told them I didn't care how I got labeled, I was running. Next, the county Republican chair asked me if I had thought about campaigning for the school board instead? I repeated that I was running for Congress.

Running for Congress is a full-time job with no pay. Fortunately, I had my military retirement, but it wasn't enough, so I would need to spend my savings to cover basic living expenses and fulfill my commitments to charities. This financial fact explains a lot about some of the people who make it through the gauntlet to serve in elected office. Only someone affluent enough to go months or even years with diminished or no income, or someone with a spouse who is the family's chief earner, or someone who is willing to suffer a financial loss or go into debt to run, can become a serious candidate.

On February 9, I announced my candidacy. The primary election was in sixty-eight days. My name recognition was probably less than 1 to 2 percent. The 2012 GOP presidential primary was also in full swing, and Rick Santorum, the former U.S. senator from Pennsylvania, was surging.

Then the military announced it was opening more combat unit support positions to women, and when Santorum was asked about this, he objected, saying it wasn't in "the best interest of men, women, or the mission." Those words were guaranteed to incite many women (including me). I was asked to appear on the morning show *Fox and Friends,* my first national interview as a candidate. I said, "When I heard this, I really just wanted to go kick him in the Jimmy." That candid fighter-pilot style response shocked the hosts and many viewers, and my comments went viral. Senator Kyl said he almost choked on his coffee as he watched. When I met Senator McCain for the first time, he told me that he laughed so hard and was now using the term all the time. We joked about "kick 'em in the Jimmy" becoming my campaign slogan, but we wanted men to vote for me without feeling as if they needed to buy a protective cup, so we decided against it.

The primary was a frenzy of visits to different groups, speaking engagements, meet-and-greets, media interviews, debates, phone calls, forums, and everything else I had no idea needed to be done as a political candidate. I had parachuted into the field, and my team and I were "building the airplane as we flew it." Somehow, we raised about $250,000, despite not being very focused on fundraising.

Although I won the ballots cast on primary day, I lost the early voting, and came in second out of four candidates. The winner then lost the special general election and decided not to run again in the fall. So now I had another primary in August and, if I won that, another general election in November.

On June 25, during a critical campaign week, my golden retriever, Penelope, fell seriously ill. I stayed with her at the vet. I brought reading material, a phone charger, a blanket, and some snacks, and made fundraising calls as I sat with her in a large crate.

Campaigning felt very much like being on a military deployment. Those of us who have served in uniform are used to performing at top speed for long hours, seven days a week, on little sleep, while still needing to think straight and communicate well. Leading a campaign team is also similar to leading a unit or a company. It is up to the leader to set the core values and establish the overall climate, culture, and vision for the team. Then a leader needs to empower each person to do their job to accomplish the mission.

I didn't realize it when I entered, but all the denigration that I had faced as a woman in the military prepared me well for being attacked, lied about, and smeared on TV, in partisan mailers, on social media, and all the other venues opponents use to try to discredit you. There were many days when I dipped into my misery database to persevere.

I told my team that campaigning is like flying a combat mission. No matter what threats appear as you fly, your ultimate goal is to reach the target to complete your mission, and you cannot lose sight of that. Similarly, in politics your target is to win the election so you can serve. Most of the personal attacks are distracting but not fatal. You can't allow yourself to focus on nuisance attacks, only on the attacks that could take you out for good. But always keep the final goal of the campaign's mission—Election Day—in mind.

Once again, I won on Election Day, but ultimately lost the race by .84% when the final votes were counted. In politics, there is no serving when you come in second. Senator Kyl told me that I would learn a lot, including a lot about myself, by running for office. It is also possible to serve and do good for others simply by running, even if in the end, you are not the one who is called to win. And while I still believed that to be 100 percent true, it sure didn't feel good to fail.

When I was approached to run again, I had to consider carefully whether working long hours nearly every day, putting my personal life on hold (not easy to date while running for Congress!), racking up big credit card balances, and being lied about and denigrated was truly the best way for me to help others. I often joked that if I didn't end up in Congress, I would work with an animal rescue organization due to my deep love for animals. I conduct ad hoc search and rescues for lost dogs around my neighborhood all the time. But it wasn't totally a joke. With animals, you can tangibly see the difference you are making on an almost daily basis, while it is definitely much harder to see progress in politics.

Nevertheless, I continued on the campaign trail, and I was encouraged. Former Defense Secretary Donald Rumsfeld, the man I had sued over the abaya, even donated to my campaign! At the end, my mom and brother flew out and made phone calls to voters. My mom would get on the phone and say, "I'm Martha's mom, and you need to vote for her." A lot of my mission-focused, purpose-driven personality I get from my mom, and in that race, she brought out hers for me.

By Election Day in 2014, I was truly ready to accept either outcome. It was a wonderful place to be. We gave it our all and left it all out on the field. Instead of feeling anxious and waiting in a back room staring at a computer as votes were reported, I was with my friends and supporters, celebrating our effort. As expected, the winner was not called that night; tens of thousands of ballots remained to be counted. I was in a better overall position than in 2012, but not ahead by enough to retain a solid lead. It was a roller-coaster ride of numbers, information, and emotions. On Friday, when I went for my run with Boomer, I believed I would lose the race by a couple of hundred votes. I would rather have lost by ten thousand.

By this point in my life, I was in a healthy place where I could grieve disappointments deeply without letting the failure define me and rise from the ashes with resilience and optimism quickly. When Sunday arrived, I was already thinking about the upside of losing. I would get my life back. I could spend more time with family, friends, and Boomer. I would have time to date. I was ready to move on.

None of these consolations was needed, however, because on Monday, the vote count shifted in my favor. By Tuesday night, it looked like I would hang on to the win. During a conference call with my team, Jeff Roe, my strategist and now a good friend, jokingly said, "The only person on this line who is now disappointed by the likelihood of victory is Martha." I won by less than .01 percent, though the race wasn't called until December 17, after a mandatory recount.

On January 6, 2015, I stood on the floor of the House of Representatives next to Sam Johnson of Texas, who was a POW in Vietnam, raised my right hand, and took the same exact oath of office that Sam and I had taken as military officers. It was a deep honor to take this oath next to an American hero.

I considered Congress to be my next service assignment, just in civilian clothes. I have a mind-set that I deploy to D.C., which in its own way is sometimes more hostile and complicated than other deployment locations!

I worked hard to represent my very diverse community and district. I flew back and forth each week when the House of Representatives was in session, roughly seventy trips per year. There are no direct flights between Washington and Tucson, so the commute is eight to nine hours door-to-door, in the best-case scenario with no delays. (I kept the same schedule in the Senate.)

I hired an amazing team to work with me in D.C. and Arizona and looked at my time as a legislator in the same way that I have every other important commitment: This could be the last two years of my life. What am I going to do with this time and opportunity to make a difference for others? We know where the two parties disagree. It's on display daily on cable TV. In a divided government, I focus on where the Venn diagrams overlap. Is there *any* common ground? With that mind-set, if something literally takes an act of Congress to fix, it needs to get through the House and the Senate, and then be signed by the president. Just like the *Schoolhouse Rock* Saturday morning cartoon I watched as a kid on how a bill becomes a law. I take a pragmatic approach to solving problems, so I look for solutions that can make it through this often brutal process. I am mindful of the political games, and I need to be alert to them to be successful, but I don't play them myself. Often I seek out other veterans on both sides of the aisle to partner with, since we start with the same core values of service to the country and others. After my freshman term, I was rated by an independent organization as the ninth most effective member of Congress out of the four hundred and thirty-five representatives due to my approach and results.

In 2016, I won reelection by 14 percent. That election night was the first, and only so far, when I definitively knew the outcome of the race. But it wasn't without drama. As I was preparing to step onstage and deliver my victory speech, one of my neighbors called to say I needed to come home immediately because water was flooding my driveway—a pipe had broken. I responded that I couldn't deal with it at that moment, and I didn't mean emotionally. My neighbors shut off the water and the fire department down the street arrived to help. My brother introduced me for my victory speech, then raced home with our cousin and another friend to try to save my furniture. While I was doing TV interviews, I was picturing water flowing through my home and wondering what had been destroyed.

Thank God (again) for Phil and Helene. I moved in with them for about three months while the damage was repaired. The flood became a kind of blessing because it gave me more time with Phil after his cancer diagnosis. Every day I spent with him was precious.

I continued to serve my constituents, but it soon became

clear that the environment had shifted dramatically after President Donald Trump was elected. My team in the state, which was bipartisan and simply wanted to serve the people in Arizona, was hounded by protesters, harassers, angry callers, and visitors. A fifty-eight-year-old man was sentenced to federal prison for threatening to kill me.

But there were well-earned successes. One of my most meaningful experiences was being a part of the Problem Solvers Caucus in the House. At the time it was twenty-three Republicans and twenty-three Democrats. We were all aware that we often didn't agree on the major issues of the day. But we worked hard to find areas where we could find some common ground. We shared tacos and beer late at night or met early in the morning over coffee. One of my best memories is the late night I sat on the floor in my office, bent over a whiteboard, working with my colleagues on a solution to stabilize the individual health insurance market. Together, all forty-six of us agreed on a unified solution. It was the way we all should picture legislators from both sides working for a common good, and there is no reason why it shouldn't happen more often.

I WAS PLANNING TO RUN for reelection in 2018 when Arizona's junior U.S. senator, Jeff Flake, announced his retirement. Many trusted people, including Senator Kyl, urged me to run for what we all knew would be a high stakes and an uphill battle. I had ten months to campaign statewide from a cold start, and I still had a full-time job in Congress. Other, more risk-averse people would have most likely taken a pass, but I followed my calling and returned to a deployment mind-set. I rarely slept in my own bed and hardly saw my close friends and Boomer, except when he could travel with me on the campaign trail. For the third time in my life, election night was not over in one night. Although I was ahead at the outset, after six days I knew I was going to lose. I called my opponent, Kyrsten Sinema, to congratulate her and wish her well. It was over. I made a little video with Boomer by my side to share my congratulations publicly. Then I got in the car with Boomer, put gas in the tank and air in a tire, grabbed some food to go, and drove myself the two hours from Phoenix to Tucson.

I was exhausted, physically and mentally, and a little in shock. Even though I had known the challenges of the race, I hadn't spent one minute contemplating losing. This isn't delusional, it is simply a better way to approach a battle. It is not helpful to ride an emotional roller coaster, where you focus on polls and attack ads and constantly wonder what the outcome might be. It would be paralyzing to fly into combat thinking only about the possibility of being shot down or to start a marathon thinking only about not finishing. Much the same is true of the mental experience of a campaign.

On December 17, Doug Ducey, the governor of Arizona, called—we talked on my cell phone while I stood in a parking lot of a restaurant where I was hosting a combined holiday, thank you, and good-bye dinner for my Congressional team. The governor asked if I would be willing to accept the appointment to serve in Arizona's other U.S. Senate seat and agree to run in 2020. That position had been held by Senator John McCain, until he tragically passed away. In the interim, Senator Kyl had agreed to return to serve in Washington, but only until the end of 2018. Under Arizona law, whoever was formally appointed would be required to run in a special election in 2020 to serve out the remainder of Senator McCain's term, and, if they won that race, then turn around and run again in 2022 to earn a full six-year term. I said yes. On January 3, 2019, I took the oath of office as Arizona's fourteenth senator.

Working in Washington, D.C. was the most frustrating thing I have done in my life. But it is very important. I had a seat at the table instead of shaking my head at the news on TV. Daily, and sometimes hourly, I prayed to release the frustration and replace it with gratitude for being given the opportunity to serve. Every time I could make a difference for someone else or give a voice to a constituent who would otherwise fail to be heard, I was grateful. It was an honor to fight for the people I represent and to focus on real results for Arizonans and their families.

One of my best Senate experiences was participating in the bipartisan weekly prayer breakfast. We prayed, sang, and one senator shared the lessons learned in their personal faith journey. It is a true place of fellowship with other senators, regardless of side, where we got to know each other's hearts. In the midst of the rancor and division in the country and D.C., that weekly breakfast has become a place of faith, not just in God but in each other to solve the challenges we face as a nation.

In public office, I also tried to stay true to myself. I was still the person who spots a stray dog and hops out of the car, at the risk of derailing my work schedule, to try to rescue that dog and reunite him or her with their family. (I'd hope for the same if Boomer ever went missing.) I've spent hours after dinner or on holidays trekking through the desert with an extra leash and treats in my hand, only at the end to hear from a constituent, "You look kind of familiar." There's nothing like the joy of a human-dog reunion, and I just can't walk or drive by a problem if I can help fix it. I did not win my hard-fought, high-stakes 2020 U.S. Senate race against another pilot, naval aviator and former astronaut Mark Kelly (husband of former Representative Gabby Giffords), but I'm deeply appreciative of the people I met and the opportunities I had. And I know I left everything on the field for Arizona.

I find it sad that I hesitated to talk here about my time serving in the House and the Senate because of the divided era we live in. Writing this book was something I had in my heart and had started doing long before I first ran for office, and I didn't want the fact that I have been a Republican senator and representative to matter much one way or the other. I also didn't want a typical political book, although I do hope that our political system can embrace some of the themes that have helped me throughout my life: Don't Walk by a Problem. Do Things Afraid. Break Barriers. Make Someone Proud. Do the Next Right Thing.

Most of all, we all need to find ways to thrive, whether in the darkness or in the light. Nothing has given me greater satisfaction than to be able to serve my country, in and out of uniform. I don't know what tomorrow will bring, but I am going to give all I have today to make a difference. To leave a legacy. To shine a light for others so that they can find their own strengths and follow their paths of purpose.

FOURTEEN

Thanksgiving in Botswana

"Put one foot in front of the other,
push through, and succeed."

I WAS FORTUNATE TO LEARN the meaning of that timeless rule, do unto others as you would have them do unto you, when I was growing up. After my dad was elected chairman of our local public school committee, he struck up a friendship with a man named Bob Fenton. Mr. Fenton was a World War II and Korean War vet, who lived alone and worked as the janitor at the Warwick School Department. Our family often invited him as a guest to share in a boisterous McSally family dinner on Sundays. Other times, my sister and I would accompany my dad to bring a Sunday meal to him. But we never dropped the meal and ran. My dad always made the time to visit and share a beer. My sister and I would amuse ourselves by choosing songs for Mr. Fenton's old player piano to play while he and my dad talked. My dad measured people by their character, not their titles or whether they had any letters for degrees after their names, and I was blessed to have his example.

My friend John follows this same rule. He is a successful entrepreneur and leader, and we have been speakers and facilitators at leadership development seminars. At one seminar, organized by another entrepreneur named Ben, the first lesson began before the program even started. John showed up wearing a janitor's uniform, with his name stitched across the chest. He set up chairs and tables and coffee. As the students arrived, he stood in their midst to see if they would even acknowledge that he was there. But they passed by him without so much as a glance or a word.

When the seminar officially began, Ben kicked things off by asking the students if anyone had noticed the person setting up the room. Did anyone even know his name? No one did. The facilitator then introduced John, the janitor, as the successful entrepreneur the students had come to meet. It made quite an impression. John wanted the group to learn that everyone plays a role in our success and to take the time to notice those around us and acknowledge their value. And to make an effort to walk a mile in someone else's shoes.

I have tried to do the same. When I was stationed in Tucson, as a squadron commander, I would have my squadron spend a Friday afternoon every three months volunteering in the community, such as helping to stock the local food bank and greet its clients. It gave our pilots and young airmen not only perspective but also a deeper connection to the community where we all lived.

Sometimes that community is also much wider than what we might expect. I never would have imagined that one of my most inspiring experiences would occur in the African nation of Botswana. During my final Air Force assignment with U.S. Africa Command, I was asked to help Botswana integrate women into its military.

Botswana is located in southern Africa. It gained its independence from the United Kingdom in 1966 and is the oldest democracy on the continent. It also is rated as the best country in Africa for fighting corruption and has one of the fastest-growing economies in the world. Yet even with this national progress, the Botswana Defense Force (BDF) did not allow women to serve in the military, unlike most of the neighboring countries.

The country's parliament had passed a law directing that women be allowed to serve, but the military kept coming up with excuses about infrastructure and logistical barriers to prevent the change. In 2007, the BDF inducted a new commander, and in his inaugural speech, he announced it was time to open up the force to women. Because of my unique experiences, the American embassy offered me up to help. Sometimes opportunities appear when you least expect them, and they bless *you* more than the other way around.

I made several trips to Botswana to mentor the first class of female officer candidates—Botswana decided it wanted to recruit female officers first, to be examples for enlisted women once they opened up their ranks.

They had solicited the candidates in a highly unusual way: an ad in the newspaper. More than twelve hundred applicants responded. Think about it: in a country where women had never served in the military before, these women were brave enough to answer the call. They had little idea of what they were getting into, but they were independent, smart, and feisty, and eager to serve. They reminded me a lot of the World War II female pilots.

After additional scrutiny and interviews, the military selected thirty trailblazers. Each woman had already obtained at least a bachelor's degree and was working in a civilian profession. But military training, and all that it involved, was going to be quite new. To make it even more challenging, these women would not be training in Botswana, which lacked the infrastructure for gender-integrated training. The commander did not want this obstacle to create further delays. He decided that the women would be sent to the East African nation of Tanzania, to train in a language, Swahili, which they did not speak, and with lethal equipment they had never seen—and to think that I was once nervous about taking paragliding lessons in German!

I had only a few days to hold our initial mentoring sessions, and I had no idea what their specific training would be like. So, I decided to use our time to prepare them generally for their roles as pioneers and leaders. Although American culture is quite different from Botswana's, military culture is universal. And the challenges they would face while breaking barriers in a previously all-male military would likely be similar to some of the dynamics I had experienced. Humans are humans, regardless of continent.

One of the simple things I told them was to take everything one day at a time, sometimes just one hour at a time. That it would be hard, but if they kept putting one foot in front of the other, they would move forward on their journey. However, simply putting one foot in front of the other was a lot more challenging for a Botswanan woman than for an American one.

Recalling my own experiences in boot camp and knowing that all military training includes intense physical conditioning and recruits need strength and stamina, I decided to give them a fitness test. Although they were young and healthy, few of them had participated in any kind of athletics, and I thought it would be helpful to put together a training regimen for them, even if it was similar to me running around my neighborhood trying to break in my combat boots before leaving for the Air Force Academy. But during our physical fitness evaluation, I looked at their footwear and grew concerned that so many of them had low-quality, ill-fitting, or worn-out athletic shoes.

As a lifelong runner, I know that having the right shoes is crucial to avoid injuries in training, but Botswana wasn't able to issue any shoes or offer a stipend to buy any, and these young women couldn't afford a high-quality pair of running shoes on their own. The happiest shopping expedition I've ever been on was when we all met at the shoe store in the mall on the evening of our last day together and nearly cleaned out its inventory. The women beamed as they carried out their new shoes, and I loved being able to have something as simple as my credit card to help set them up for success.

My admiration for these incredible young women grew as we spent our days together. They told me that many of their families had reacted to the news that they were joining the military with a combination of pride and a little fear. That's about how my family responded when I announced that I wanted to become a fighter pilot. But some spoke about how their male and female loved ones did not support the path they had chosen. Instead, they were told to focus on finding a husband and having children. But even when they lacked support, they were undeterred and remained humbled and honored to be selected for such a history-making role.

I hugged them all and wished them well in their training, knowing it wouldn't be an easy road. Before they departed for Tanzania, I received word from the U.S. embassy that one woman had died, and there were allegations that she had been poisoned by her boyfriend because he was opposed to her becoming an Army officer. It was a stark reminder of the massive cultural barriers they were breaking, with far higher resistance than a ranting voice mail left on an answering machine or a "Ka-Ching" shouted by some insecure fighter pilots.

When the women completed their training, I returned for the ceremony to welcome these new officers into the Botswana Defense Force. Their training stories were harrowing. One recruit suffered severe injuries and had to return home. (She recovered and later served as a civilian in the BDF.) The rest succeeded, under very challenging circumstances.

I learned that Tanzania's military selects its officers from the ranks of enlisted soldiers, which means that all of their officer cadets have already served in the military and know the basics of marching, drills, weapons, and day-to-day military life. But these Botswanan women were civilians experiencing both the military and military training for the first time. They had no basic knowledge to draw upon, instead it was total immersion. (It made my experiences in basic training at the Air Force Academy seem like a country club outing.)

They had received no exposure on how to handle, shoot, clean, disassemble, and assemble weapons and had to largely figure it out themselves. They proudly shared that in order to pass the training course, they were required to climb Mount Kilimanjaro with no support, no food, and little water, making it to the top and back down in two days. (My "easy" trek to the summit and back had taken six days and had the benefit of guides, porters, and huts.) They told me how valuable their new running shoes were, and how they also served to remind them of my words of encouragement to put one foot in front of the other, push through, and succeed. They overcame extreme obstacles and persevered to earn their commissions. I could not have been prouder of them.

Their induction ceremony was scheduled to be held around Thanksgiving, so when I arrived, I invited them to a celebratory meal at a local restaurant and explained how, on this American holiday, many families ask each person at the table to reflect on something they are thankful for. We may not have had turkey and stuffing, but as we went around the table, their sincere sentiments of gratitude made it one of the most memorable holidays in my life.

Ten years later, during Thanksgiving week 2018, right after I had lost the bruising Arizona Senate race, I received an email from one of the Botswana pioneers:

Col McSally

Good evening ma'am. My name is [. . .] of the
Botswana Defence Force, one of the first 30 female
officer cadets our military employed.

I watched the news and was rooting for you during
the recent mid-term elections. You fought a good
fight ma'am.

The upcoming Thanksgiving Holiday serves as
a reminder of the Thanksgiving you shared with us
back in 2008. In my country we don't really have
thanksgiving as a holiday but each time that time of
the year comes around, I remember that one in 2008.

Your words continue to inspire us ma'am and we
will never forget you. When things get tough we are
reminded to "put one foot in front of another" and
that being a pioneer isn't easy.

I wish you well in all your future endeavors.
Happy Thanksgiving ma'am.

I was proud to learn that she had achieved the rank of
captain, but just as important, I was moved by how she had
taken the time to offer such a thoughtful act of compassion.
It meant so much to me at a moment when I needed to be reminded of real victories. Throughout the years, I also heard
from a number of the Botswanan officers, who addressed
me as "Mum"—I guess "Momma Mac" was the right call
sign for me after all.

When I first arrived in Botswana, I thought that I needed

to whip into shape some civilian girls who might not be tough enough for the uncertain and rough journey ahead. Instead, much as I had with Amy and the female World War II pilots, I found an unexpected sisterhood. I grew to love and be inspired by these trailblazers who overcame far more difficult barriers in their country, lives, and military service than I could even imagine. It made me thankful for the challenges I had experienced, so I could offer a light to these extraordinary pioneers as they set out on their own paths.

AT THE SAME TIME AS I had been meeting with the women, I had also been working with senior male leaders of the BDF to plan for their forces to integrate women. Initially, the central concerns had been about preparing the women, but now it was apparent that they had more than risen to the challenge. The men and the institution were the ones lagging behind. Despite all the ideas I had shared and discussions we conducted during a seminar with the senior leadership a full year before, very little had been done to follow up and be ready to accept women (sound a little bit familiar?).

Among some of the basics that had been missed, no one had briefed all commanders on anything related to the arrival of women into their units to ensure a professional culture. No policies had been created with regard to training on sexual harassment, assault, fraternization, and professional relationships, let alone preparing the male soldiers who were about to incorporate a female officer into their unit for the first time, not unlike my initial A-10 squadron when I first joined. I asked to meet with the defense chief, who had the vision and courage to open up the military to women, and he gave me full authority to devise a plan.

I gave the BDF a list of policies they needed to create, with examples from our U.S. policies. I led additional seminars with their senior leaders and helped them to think about and devise their own standards for everything from physical fitness and hairstyles to professionalism. I also flew around the country and conducted seminars at several bases. It was slow, but each time I returned, more progress had been made.

During one visit, I was able to meet the newest group of female officer candidates, who were participating in gender-integrated training alongside their male officer counterparts inside Botswana, a much better plan than sending them to another country. As in America, I discovered that some men were champions of giving women opportunities to serve and lead in the military. They were my best partners, because in the end I would return home, but they could lead and make integration successful. As with the U.S. military, there were also some insecure men, who were determined to resist integration at all costs. The vast majority of men were bystanders, who could be encouraged to go along with either side. I wanted to give the BDF and the women the best chance to succeed by providing the bystanders with the reasons and motivation to choose honor and professionalism and inclusivity.

In 2013, Botswana accepted its first female enlisted personnel, and in 2019, its first female pilots earned their wings. Progress takes time, and I feel so fortunate to have participated in a small way.

Other embassies in Africa heard about my efforts with Botswana and asked if I could lead seminars addressing professionalism, sexual harassment, sexual assault, and other issues related to women in the military. I happily said yes and conducted seminars with military leaders and female troops in Swaziland, Sierra Leone, and Lesotho, where I flew alongside First Lieutenant Malefane, the Lesotho Defense Force's first female pilot, in her cockpit.

Perhaps the most challenging environment in which to have a gender-integrated, professional military was Swaziland, also known as Eswatini. Swaziland is a beautiful, very small country completely surrounded by South Africa. Ruled by an absolute monarchy, it is also a country where men may have multiple wives, and where young girls perform a reed dance each year in part designed to "preserve their chastity." At the time I was there, Swaziland had the highest HIV/AIDS infection rate in the world, more than 25 percent of the population aged fifteen to forty-nine. The poverty rate was also high, and the military was considered a good-paying job. The U.S. embassy explained to me that the military was struggling with managing male officers, who treated the female enlisted barracks as a brothel.

One of Swaziland's female leaders shared a few of her own harrowing encounters, which made many of my difficult experiences seem small. I was inspired by her resolve and grit and her tough-as-nails attitude. I decided to focus my efforts on discussing with leaders, male and female, how, when you put on the uniform, you become a part of something greater than yourself. You take an oath of office and should set an example for society on what honor, service, and integrity means. You choose to sacrifice, serve, and fight to defend your country, with the goal of becoming selfless leaders, who do not abuse their power over anyone.

When women (or men) are being mistreated, it is usually symptomatic of larger issues: abuse of power, corruption, unprofessional relationships, favoritism, take your pick. Change those, and you will likely improve everyone's circumstances. It is a difficult mission, but I have faith it can be done, one person at a time. But to dismantle barriers like these, we have to first recognize and understand them.

In the U.S. military, we often use concrete barriers to protect our bases. During a training exercise in Arizona, a team was told to move a wide ring of barriers. It was a dark, moonless night. The team counted the barriers and decided how many cranes and flatbed trailers they would need to lift and transport them to their new locations. Working through the night, they called in the necessary equipment.

As the sun rose and the armada of heavy equipment arrived, someone on the ground noticed that nearly half the barriers had already been moved. The team hastily gathered. In the distance, they saw one young lieutenant pushing a barrier as if he were Superman. Running toward him, the team realized their mistake. In the darkness, no one had gone out to inspect the barriers up close. They were all identically shaped plastic shells filled with water, not concrete. All that had been required was to open the valve and let the water drain to transform them into lightweight, plastic shells. In the darkness, they looked like something they were not. The same lesson applies to many of the seemingly heavy and immovable barriers in our own lives. Barriers are for breaking. Don't be afraid to give them a push.

Epilogue

Integrity First

"You may not go off to fly attack
jets, but you have your own
amazing destiny."

NOT LONG AGO, I RETURNED to Rhode Island to celebrate my mother's eighty-fifth birthday and revisit some of the places that held so much meaning in my childhood. Back then, the waters where my dad taught me to pilot our boat under that low bridge and out to sea seemed incredibly vast and scary. Now, they were shockingly small and unbelievably calm. Facing that first journey to a new job alone, while my dad watched down from heaven, that little girl suddenly found herself as the captain of her ship. But to achieve that freedom, I first had to conquer my fear.

I am grateful that I was taught and learned to do things afraid. If we wait for life to be perfect in fit, form, or function before we step forward—if we want the gauge to read "comfortable" before we walk through a doorway or push down a runway—we will never move from the place we are. So, don't hesitate. Don't look down! Do things afraid, and in time, the challenge will not seem as vast and scary. Neither will the next, greater challenge.

Just as fighter pilots do, we need to craft a flight plan and develop strong tactics to get to our next destination. Training is invaluable. Chair flying in a place of safety allows us to prepare for the real task. It teaches us to keep our wings level when faced with small things, so we can handle the unexpected.

Few sorties in life are short or direct. Instead, we fly from one navigation point to another and then another, before we reach our target. Facing the daunting challenge of a triathlon—whether a real one or a metaphorical one—we can fall prey to self-defeat before we start. So, make a plan and focus on some milestones. Concentrate on getting to that next water station. Along the way, trust your loyal wingmen, and have faith. Inexplicably, during the times when you find yourself overpowered and want to quit, hands will reach out and lift you up.

Could I have known that a colonel who arrived unaware of my struggle in Saudi Arabia would become my die-hard defender? Could I have known the Air Force's top leader would intervene in an abusive, callous bureaucracy and make things right? Could I have known that my next-door neighbors Helene and Phil would be my rock? Could I have known that four-legged companions would add so much love and depth to my life? Could I have ever predicted that the president and the entire Congress would one day say, "We agree," when I chose to not walk by a problem that required liberating American servicewomen from outrageous rules in a foreign land? Could I ever have known how many people would teach me so much and how many would give to me so generously? Could I have known that my mother, a widow with five children, would keep me on track and become my greatest cheerleader? Could I have known I would rise from the loss of my father to be the nation's first woman to fly a fighter jet in combat? Could I have known I would survive a predator in high school and rape by a military superior yet find a way to forgive and move forward to achieve the honor of becoming the first female Air Force officer to command a fighter squadron and later become a U.S. senator?

No matter what, expect miracles and blessings! Until they arrive, thrive in the darkness knowing that God-sent wingmen will come and that your training was worthwhile. Tap into your misery database, and never let go. Flying a combat mission that saves others in war may require you to fly through the fires of hell. Accept this reality and keep your eyes on the target. Do the next right thing. And when you are injured and unsure, take time to heal and reset. Call a knock-it-off to restore yourself and your toehold when it's evident that you should.

Without any hesitation, I have shared these deeply personal experiences and insights from my life's course with the hope of encouraging you in your own journey. It doesn't matter who you are, your age, background, or where you are in life. There is, however, one more key insight. I saved a discussion of an essential principle that bathes every line you've read. It demands its own spotlight.

"Integrity First" is the first core value of the Air Force, and I have made it the central core value of my life. Integrity means following the truth in both the small things and the big things. There's no difference. Don't cheat on your taxes. When you are late, don't fudge and say you are down the street when you are still a mile or more away. Maintaining your integrity in the small things builds a pattern that will help you keep it when the stakes are high.

Integrity also means being true to your word. Say what you mean and mean what you say. If you say you are going to do something, then make it happen. If for some reason circumstances change and you can't follow through, then communicate and be clear about what you will do next or have the back-up plan. Most of all, integrity means doing the right thing even when no one is watching. It means being true and trustworthy, whatever our path and whatever our goals.

Integrity is universally viewed as something that is manifested externally, being moral and honest in our outward conduct. This is especially needed in today's world where so many believe that winning justifies any means, and, to achieve victory, lies, distortion, and slander are required.

There is, however, another side to integrity. Integrity is not only outward, it is also inward—and these two components meet at the core of who we are. We can understand the need to be honest and morally true in the things we do. But it is also important to recognize that we need integrity within ourselves.

One of my heroes is a famous fighter pilot, John Boyd. He spoke about reaching a fork in the road, and the choice that every military aviator faces, but it applies to us all. The first choice of path is to "be somebody." These are the people who simply go along and get along. They get promoted and receive the better assignments, but also are more likely to compromise themselves and forget their friends.

The second path allows you to "do something." The people who choose to "do something" may not be promoted, they may not receive the best assignments, and they certainly may not be a favorite of their superiors. But, Boyd said, you "won't have to compromise yourself. You will be true to your friends and to yourself. And your work might make a difference." My dad also believed in "do something," as he wrote all those years ago to my mom.

All my life, I have been called to *do something*, rather than *be somebody*, to have a purpose to my work and to make a difference. To make my dad proud. But I have also tried to balance that drive to do something with the knowledge that every day is a gift. We are all sons and daughters of God with unique purposes and paths to reach our potential. Each of us goes through difficult times and feels fear. Nonetheless, we all can freely choose to live life to its fullest, as we were created to do. Living with compassion and gratitude is also its own reward. Everyone has challenges, and everyone can help someone else who crosses their path, in ways large and small. Extend your compassion to all living creatures. Volunteer for causes you believe in. Walk alongside someone facing circumstances similar to ones that you have walked through in the past. Shine a light for their path ahead. Buy someone who needs them a new pair of shoes.

I also hope you don't feel sympathy for me. I've experienced tragedy and difficulties, but those have been more than balanced by kindness and opportunity. Most of all, I want you to know that if I can overcome obstacles, you can, too. You may not go off to fly attack jets, but you have your own amazing destiny. There is a spectacular adventure out there for all of us who pass through deep darkness to arrive at a sunlit victory. We just need to embrace an inward integrity and be faithful to the belief that each of us can achieve seemingly impossible feats.

In Rhode Island, I thought about the special times when my dad would take me to dig for clams. Back then, in the sparkling water, the clams were abundant. Dad and I would hunt them with our feet. We waded in, digging our toes deep into the sand until we struck upon a hard, rough shell. Each time I would scream, "I found one!" No doubt my dad was amused by the freshness I felt with each discovery. Finding a clam never became old, no matter how many buckets we filled during the summer.

Forty years later, my sister-in-law and I paddled kayaks to the same clamming area where I made those precious memories with my dad. After sitting in quiet contemplation, I reflexively got out of the kayak and waded into the familiar water. I pictured my dad's hand around mine as my feet probed the sand. I didn't find anything at first. Just as Mary said, "You need to think of your dad," I felt a clam. With the passion I had as a child, I exclaimed, "I found one!" I'm sure my dad in heaven heard his grown-up girl and smiled. Trust me, the simplest joy can lift us all!

Few things are more beautiful to an aviator than that

moment when we break free of the dark, turbulent, and menacing clouds and soar into the bright sky and sunlight above. I trust and pray, and confidently believe, that you too can soar. That you will do amazing things and maybe even change the rules that keep so many others on the ground.

You are cleared for takeoff—I dare you to fly!

Addendum

Peace, Joy, and Gratitude

FOR MOST OF 2020, AMERICANS were grounded. The routines of life and simple joys we took for granted were suddenly undone by a virus. From health worries, to losing loved ones (often without being able to hold them and say goodbye), to the isolation of our most vulnerable, the loss of jobs, the shutdown of small businesses, kids being out of school—in some way, everyone's lives have been upended.

I finished writing this book Thanksgiving weekend 2019, having no idea what our country would be facing when *Dare to Fly* was released in May 2020. Yet the lessons in these pages—such as overcoming fear, thriving through the darkness, becoming resilient, being strengthened by adversity, and finding your faith—are even more relevant during difficult and uncertain times. At the end of 2019, the words that God put on my heart for my 2020 sticky notes were peace, joy, and gratitude. Time and again, throughout this year, those three words were exactly the ones I needed to hear.

When the pandemic hit, I was deeply moved by the extent of the calamity—along my street, across my state, throughout our entire nation. The suffering was everywhere: hospitals, nursing homes, families, small businesses, schools, seniors. I was honored to be able to cast a vote as a US senator for federal aid, but I was also fortunate to have an emergency savings account of my own. I'm not wealthy, but this was an emergency. I'm grateful that I was in a position to write checks to neighbors and friends who were hurting and able to buy grocery cards to hand out when I saw a need. With much of the country shut down, I volunteered to help distribute food and supplies. I temporarily stopped all fundraising for my senate campaign and instead personally asked my donors to give to those who were struggling. I am thankful I had these opportunities to help; throughout my life, I have been blessed to have others help me along the way. I have also been deeply inspired by the compassion, innovation, and creativity I witnessed from neighbors, companies, churches, universities, and nonprofits to fill gaps for vital PPE for essential workers, provide daycare and meals for healthcare heroes, grocery shop for the vulnerable, and so much more. What a joy to see this horrible challenge bring out the best in people.

The year 2020 has been personally difficult for me, too. The week before Christmas, my uncle Dave, my mom's younger brother, died from COVID at the age of 82. And

in July, my fifty-eight-year-old brother, Martin, unexpectedly passed away (although not from COVID). I got the
tragic news and flew from Washington to meet my other
siblings so we could tell our eighty-five-year-old mom that
her son was dead. The pandemic had already been cruel to
seniors like my mom; as with so many around the country, she had been isolated and in lockdown for months. State
rules allowed us to have a small service with restrictions. As
I had at Martin's wedding, I sang at his funeral, an honor I
never wanted to experience. But in 2020, many other families didn't have even this bit of comfort.

The last time Martin and I spoke, he had called me to say
he read this book, really enjoyed it, and was proud of me.
He told me that some memories I shared were painful to
read, and he learned things about me that he didn't know.
He wondered if he was the brother who took me on the
practice run in that little dingy before I piloted it solo to my
first job. I thank God we had that conversation, especially
since, like so many others this year, I didn't get to say goodbye. Martin left three children, the youngest of whom is the
same age as Martin was when our dad died. I pray they find
their paths of healing, resilience, and faith. This untimely
loss has reminded me again that every day is truly a gift.

As I write this, I am also experiencing the disappointment of losing my US Senate campaign to continue serving
Arizona. I received the second-largest number of votes ever
for a statewide candidate in Arizona, but in politics there
are no prizes for second place. I knew when I accepted an

appointment to the Senate that it would be a high-risk, high-consequence, high-purpose mission. But I chose to serve and was blessed by the opportunity. This bittersweet experience gives me a chance to follow my own advice and live the principles in this book. Indeed, going through another challenging chapter makes me more confident in the value of those principles.

I have a heart of gratitude for the opportunity to have been a US senator—and one of only six hundred and seventy-seven Americans to serve in both chambers of Congress—especially at such a critical time. I am so inspired and humbled by the many wingmen who joined me in the fight. I'm thankful to have passed meaningful legislation on issues that include veterans' mental health and sexual assault in the military. I met amazing people, including four Navajo World War II code talkers on the Navajo Nation. I am also proud that, despite this era of division, I left the US Senate tied for the most bills signed into law and ranked as the sixth most bipartisan senator, because I joined with those on both sides of the aisle to find common ground for the common good.

But no one needs a title to serve or to make a difference. When I went to cast my election ballot, as I walked through the parking garage, a man came up to me. "Thank you for helping to find our sweet girl," he said with tears in his eyes. He was talking about his daughter's dog, who had gone missing over Thanksgiving 2019 (the same weekend I was finalizing this book!). For days I helped comb our neighborhood and the desert, put up signs, chase leads, follow tracks, and place food and water to help rescue their beloved dog. We talked about the dog and how she whimpered in his arms when they were reunited, and he showed me pictures of his new grandchild. It was a moment of neighbors helping neighbors, at a time when we have all come to realize how much we depend on each other.

That is what matters: doing the next right thing, whether in your home, on your block, in your state, or for the nation. Every day, we are given the opportunity to be someone else's wingman, to look out and care for them. Now more than ever, I think of the meaning of President Theodore Roosevelt's words, which I have carried with me for my entire adult life: even if we fail at times, remember that we are daring greatly. We are daring to fly. Never will our place be with those timid souls who knew neither victory nor defeat.

As you take flight, I hope you will also remember that every moment, every day, each new chapter of our lives is a gift. Start them with peace, joy, and gratitude.

Author's Note

TO RECOUNT EVENTS in this book, I have been greatly helped by contemporaneous notes and other documentation. Select conversations have been reconstructed based on those notes and memories. All emails and additional written communications that are quoted are from direct printouts or copies of those writings. In addition, many of the individuals involved have generously shared their personal recollections with me. The material on John Boyd is derived from Robert Coram's biography, *Boyd: The Fighter Pilot Who Changed the Art of War* (Back Bay Books, 2004).

Acknowledgments

FOR SOMEONE WHO LIKES to set and achieve goals, publishing this book was a goal that eluded me for many years. I am deeply grateful to so many people who inspired, encouraged, prodded, and helped me finally to complete it.

I am thankful for all the incredible people who have been part of my life so far, many but not all of whom are mentioned in this book. My dad is my inspiration. Although he left this world way too soon, he gave me an example of service, hard work, and compassion. My mom showed me how to persevere and function in the midst of profound loss. I am so proud of her and love her dearly. My sister, Mary Kaitlin, and brothers, Martin, Michael, and Mark, each have taught me important lessons, spoken and unspoken, as they charted the seasons of life before me. They have loved me and encouraged me as I marched to the beat of my own drum, and I will always be their baby sister.

I wouldn't have survived this far without the unconditional love of the furry, four-legged angels in my life. You can make it through nearly anything if you come home to the love of a dog who brings smiles, joy, and a coat to dry all tears.

I am blessed to have had so many amazing people, who were instrumental in various roles on my journey. They include true friends like Phil and Helene, extraordinary bosses, spiritual leaders, and mentors like the Women Airforce Service pilots.

It was the highest honor of my life to wear the uniform of the United States Air Force and command men and women in combat. I remain inspired and humbled by those with whom I served, and the daily sacrifices they and their families made to keep us safe.

I am grateful for God's grace always, including His hand in the process of writing this book. The journey of writing, editing, and publishing a book was unexpectedly painful at times, but ultimately resulted in another layer of healing. Recounting stories from decades past evoked tears and laughter. My resolve and faith were strengthened as I thought about and wrote down insights from these life experiences, which I hope will inspire you to find your own courage, faith, and determination to survive, thrive, and break barriers for others.

This project spanned many years, with fits and starts and versions galore. I am eternally grateful for the amazingly talented Lyric Winik, particularly for getting my fighter pilot stories and insights into a format that civilians could appreciate without losing my voice. Thanks to Matt Latimer at Javelin for believing in the value of this project and for being a great advocate. I am so thankful to Mauro DiPreta, Senior Vice President and Executive Editor at William Morrow, for taking a leap of faith and believing in the vision of this book, as well as for his wise and thoughtful direction to guide it to its final form. In addition, thanks to the entire team at William Morrow/HarperCollins for their support and hard work to get this book to press.

Thanks to Stan Moser who urged me to write a book almost two decades ago and patiently prodded me to bring it to fruition. Matthew Scully was incredibly helpful with ideas and edits to early versions of the book, introduced me to Lyric, and offered finishing touches to strengthen the final product. Major General (ret.) Larry Stutzriem offered exceptional comments and edits to all versions, especially the epilogue. When I asked Colonel (ret.) Mike Millen to fact check my flying references, he generously stepped up to provide extraordinarily strong, detailed feedback and edits to many iterations of the whole manuscript. Thanks as well to B. C. Winik for his very helpful design contributions.

Finally, I am grateful to you, the reader, who, for whatever reason, decided to pick up this book. I am humbled you chose my stories and what I learned as a fellow sojourner in life. I don't have it all figured out. None of us do. But I pray that some insights I learned on how to overcome fear, barriers, and tragedies to find my courage and purpose will be encouraging to you on your amazing journey.